CARDIAC ARREST

A TACTICAL GUIDE ON HOW TO HANDLE UNLAWFUL POLICE STOPS

by Royce Russell, Esq.

Cardiac Arrest, A Tactical Guide on How to Handle Unlawful Police
Stops Published by: C&G Enterprises Unlimited, LLC

© 2010 Royce Russell, Esq.

CardiacArrestBookLaunch@gmail.com

Cover by Creative Genius

Book Layout by ShinyRocketDesign

ISBN-13: 978-0-9976400-2-1

DEDICATION

This tactical guide is dedicated to the 13-year-old African American teenage girl who was traveling home from cheerleading practice and used her school train pass to access the train but was falsely arrested. The name of that then teen will remain nameless but that experience has been a part of her life forever and has shaped how she raised her son and daughter and her view of the criminal justice system as a potential juror.

The story unfolds as follows: the young lady was traveling home from cheerleading practice and used her train pass, within the lawful limit; however, when she proceeded through the turnstile and walked onto the platform, a plain clothes male asked her to come to him. As you can predict, this young African American female refused the male's request. She proceeded to walk down the platform positioning herself for the arrival of the train when this same male abruptly approached the young lady and grabbed her and said, "I told you to come here." Frightened and speechless, the young lady froze as she was thrown onto the station's platform and dragged into, what appeared to be, a bathroom.

While alone in this bathroom, the male handcuffed the young lady as he used his radio to summon assistance. It was at this time the young lady realized the white male who had accosted her was a transit police officer. The officer never inquired with the token booth clerk how this young lady had entered the train station, given that the clerk had to buzz you onto the train platform by way of buzzing you through the turnstile or gate.

Naive to the criminal justice system and wanting to put this horrific experience behind them, the family allowed their daughter to enter a plea agreement to have the case dismissed. In review of this case, which resulted in the case being dismissed and sealed, clearly this teen was a victim of a FALSE ARREST and EXCESSIVE FORCE. If she were more knowledgeable about her rights, then she could have pursued a lawsuit against the officer and the police department.

This experience has stayed with this teen for decades and has shaped the way she views police, the criminal justice system, whether she wants to participate as a juror, her mental state in that capacity and, most importantly, how she has raised her kids. The sad truth is that the above after effects of FALSE ARREST and EXCESSIVE FORCE are not uncommon and it is, in my humble opinion, even more profound than I can articulate.

To that naive teenager who experienced what social media is capturing every day, I wish I were present to protect you but hopefully this Tactical Guide will serve as protection for your children and others.

FOREWORD

In every area of life there are obstacles we face. In some instances, we are fortunate enough to receive instruction, guidance or preparation that allow us to successfully navigate these constant challenges. However, in black and brown communities, the same entity sworn to assist, to "Protect and Serve" all, regardless of color, economic status, gender or location, is the same entity that poses the most threat. These eminent threats to black and brown bodies extend to losses of freedom and of life itself. It's unfortunate that in many encounters with law enforcement, it is almost impossible for an unequipped, ill-informed member of the black or brown community to escape the ordeal unscathed.

As we continuously hear of the unjustified and illegal stops of members of our community, as we continue to read about the false arrest and destruction of the lives of our youth, as we constantly turn on our televisions and radios and see or hear of one of our brethren senselessly killed at the hands of those that are sworn to protect us, it is an absolute necessity for everyone that may have an encounter with police to equip themselves with the information provided in Cardiac Arrest.

Cardiac Arrest is a navigational guide for survival and recording encounters with law enforcement. The need for members of communities of color to be armed with this vital information is a MUST due to the criminalization and dehumanization of these communities by law enforcement and the judicial system. The ability and willingness of Royce Russell to draw from his childhood experiences, time as a prosecutor and his selfless work as a civil rights attorney has enabled him to construct this well-needed and overdue guide for survival. As our youth, young adults, men and women, attempt to play, live, work and contribute positively to their communities they are in constant threat of unnecessary/unlawful encounters with law enforcement.

I would like to thank Royce Russell for using and sharing his knowledge, experience and expertise to educate the public on a very serious issue that has plagued our community. His selflessness has allowed him to produce and develop a well thought out and comprehensive guide to navigating and surviving encounters with the police. This must-read guide will give the reader the information needed to protect themselves and loved ones from the crisis that has over taken the community.

Julian D. Harper
Ret. NYPD Lieutenant
Co-founder of 100 Blacks in Law Enforcement Who Care

Royce and I met during our college years where we forged a friendship that is over 30 years in the making. Both raised in the South Bronx and later working within the NYC criminal justice system, our deepest connection is that we are fathers to young black men. As a former law enforcement officer, I have observed and encountered many of the situations that are detailed in Cardiac Arrest and strongly recommend this book be mandatory reading in all black and brown homes.

The substance in Cardiac Arrest is delicate, but very necessary in communities of color where our voices are seldom heard and our lives are often devalued. Cardiac Arrest is the perfect guide for people of color when confronted with the lack of respect and effective communication by the police.

Royce remains a staunch advocate for civil justice and his unwavering commitment and altruism to the disenfranchised is beyond reproach. His firsthand knowledge of the subject matter through work and personal life experiences make him a credible and wealthy source of information.

I'm confident that Cardiac Arrest will make a positive impact by empowering the defenseless and giving voices to the underrepresented. And maybe some police officers can read it and see things through the lenses of the marginalized? Maybe.

Manny Ramirez
NYPD Detective (Retired)

TABLE OF CONTENTS

INTRODUCTION: "THE PEOPLE HAVE SPOKEN"

Before writing *Cardiac Arrest*, I conducted an informal focus group. I asked people of color whether a book that will assist in managing an UNLAWFUL POLICE STOP would be of interest given the estranged relationship between the police and multicultural communities.

Here are some of the responses:

"Yeah just what I need; I can put this in my glove compartment, to ensure I get home alive."
Darryl, an African American male, from the "Boogie Down Bronx"-Age 38

"Sounds good, but will it work?"
Rosa, a Latino female from "Harlem USA"-Age 18

"My man, this should be part of a civic course."
T-Black, an African American male from "DA Bronx" -Age 43

"Give me your card just in case I need you."
Harlem Barber, Age 38

"My husband is a police officer and he was almost shot by his fellow officers while working undercover; this book is necessary because anyone can be a victim of a misguided and over zealous officer."
Latino Woman, Age 32

"I got beat down last week; maybe had I read this book I could have avoided the beating . . . but I know I did not totally control the outcome." *<said laughing>*
Rob, a Latino/African American from Queens-Age 18

"Nothing can really prevent what sometimes appears to be the inevitable, but I look forward to the read and the insight."
Smokie from Detroit, Age 40

"Only time will tell."
Tony from PA, Age 63

"Why stop with this book – create a DVD."
Kathy, CA. Age 44

The purpose of this book is to better prepare people of color, more specifically African Americans, Latinos, and other brown men and women, on how to deal with police encounters. What do you do when a police officer "UNLAWFULLY" stops you and asks you for identification or a driver's license or asks you where you are going or coming from. What is the "Right Response" or "Action to Take"? WHAT ARE THE RULES OF ENGAGEMENT? Rules of Engagement are the ways in which I manage a scenario that will ensure my safety and alert the police officer that I know my rights while retrieving information from the officer to file a complaint or commence a lawsuit against him/her for his/her misconduct. Whether the law enforcement person is male, female, state trooper, detective, undercover, or a cop in uniform on patrol, the rules of engagement are the same.

In an era where people of color are being subjected to police misconduct from simple harassment, battery and assault to wrongful death, we as people of color must be prepared. As of July 5, 2016, more than 1,096 people have died at the hands of the police. The Washington Post reports 908 people have been shot and killed by police. By July 5, 2016, of the 908-1,096 people killed by police, African Americans were killed at a rate of 5.38 deaths per million people. Latinos were 2.4, Whites were 2.13 and Asian/others were .78. The shocking untold story is Native Americans represent 5.49 of deaths at the hands of the police.

In recent cases, police were not criminally charged and if charged not convicted and if convicted never sentenced to prison. Unfortunately, there are numerous examples within the African American community. I have listed a few cases below.

* In the case of Jamar Clark's wrongful death in Minnesota, the Officer was not criminally indicted, despite the overwhelming factors that should have led to an indictment. As a result, the powers that be in Minnesota decided to abandon the grand jury system, which compromises the pursuit of justice. The grand jury is a panel of the citizens of the community that decide whether enough evidence exists to proceed with criminal charges against the accused and in this case, it was police officers.

* In the case of Eric Gardner's videoed wrongful death in Staten Island, New York, he was choked to death while unarmed and not resisting the police. In this case the grand jury decided against indicting the officers and therefore they walked free from criminal charges. However, in a civil case for wrongful death, his family was awarded 5.9 million dollars.

* In the case of Ramarley Graham's wrongful death case in New York, the police killed Graham in front of his grandmother and 6-year-old brother as he stood next to them unarmed. In this case the grand jury indicted the officers, but the Supreme Criminal Court Judge dismissed the indictment and those officers walked free. However, in a civil case for wrongful death, his family was awarded 3.9 million dollars.

* In the case of Freddie Gray in Baltimore, Maryland, he died in police custody as he was handcuffed and placed into a police van with no seatbelt and was violently tossed about the van while being recklessly driven by the police, which resulted in his wrongful death. Here, three officers were tried and none convicted. However, in a civil case for wrongful death, Baltimore awarded his family approximately 6.4 million dollars.

* In the case of Akai Gurley in Brooklyn, NY, the Officer was found guilty but was sentenced to 5 years of probation and 800 hours of community service. However, in a civil case for wrongful death, his family was awarded over 4 million dollars.

* From 2014 to June 2017, NYC has paid close to 200 million dollars to people wrongfully convicted of crimes and in every settlement the city disclaims wrong doing.

* On or about November 29, 2017, the case of Philando Castile, in the State of Minnesota, was settled for 3 million dollars. In his case, Castile announced he had a gun, never reached for it and was fatally shot in front of his girlfriend and 4-year-old daughter.

* April 6, 2017, NYC paid Phabo Sefolosha, an NBA player, 4 million dollars for EXCESSIVE FORCE.

Unfortunately, there are too many examples to place on a spreadsheet or chart that could truly capture the pervasive incidents of police misconduct and all the UNLAWFUL POLICE STOPS by law enforcement within communities of color. As there are laws in every society and codes of conduct in every profession, there also exists a code of conduct, rules, guidelines or words of wisdom for civilians when engaged with the police. This especially holds true for UNLAWFUL POLICE STOPS. This book will serve as your survival guide. No code of conduct or rules of the road are fool proof but being a passive victim to UNLAWFUL POLICE STOPS or EXCESSIVE FORCE is not an option. The title *Cardiac Arrest* reflects the feeling that overwhelms most when stopped by the police. Your heart starts to beat faster and faster, the palms of your hands become sweaty, and you start to become nervous as your heart is racing as if it is going to jump out your chest. Whether it is the fear of the unknown or the fear for others present, the reaction is most likely the same. This is the life of a person of color as it relates to police encounters. A heart attack is exactly what could happen when the police stop a person of color. Your heart briefly stops and thoughts of your life pass by; thoughts of being arrested/handcuffed and not making it home alive become more of your reality as you engage with the Officer who stopped you. You pray to and maybe even curse at your God during the whole UNLAWFUL POLICE STOP. And, when it is over hopefully you are thanking that same God you cursed.

Hopefully this guide, which is based on my life experiences as an African American male raised in the Bronx, "Fort Apache", New York City coupled with the lessons I learned as a civil rights/criminal defense attorney and a prosecutor, will assist you in managing an UNLAWFUL POLICE STOP. Such encounters can cause you to feel powerless, anxious, scared, helpless and infuriated all at once and leave you speechless and looking for redress and inevitably for someone to be fired. This guide will suggest how to handle the stop and how to file a complaint or a lawsuit afterwards.

As an attorney I have walked with clients through their experience of being a victim of false arrest and excessive force. I have been successful in regaining their power and self-respect by fighting for their rights when their civil rights have been violated. Such civil rights include freedom of speech; the right to be secure and free from any illegal search and seizure whether it is your person, or your property being searched or seized; the right from and against cruelty; and excessive force-false arrest. Practicing in the area of civil rights-false arrest/excessive force is a substantial part of my body of work, which inspired this book.

By **ROYCE RUSSELL, ESQ**

WHERE MY STORY BEGINS... ST. MARY'S

It is often said that everyone is entitled to an opinion, however, what is more profound is whether or not that opinion is grounded in facts or experiences that make the opinion worthy of listening to or following. My tools of the trade to successfully managing an "UNLAWFUL POLICE STOP" is grounded on my experiences as a Black male growing up in the South Bronx, particularly an area called "Fort Apache", and being an attorney practicing in the area of false arrest and police brutality for over a decade. The area of the Bronx where I grew up was referred to as "Fort Apache", a no-nonsense, hard as rock, survival of the fittest environment and, whether we recognized it or not, consisted of poor and working poor folks. I remember the day I realized money was only one color (green) and not multi-colored (food stamps). Thanks to my parents' work ethic, we were able to survive without food stamps and never looked back. Fort Apache, the Bronx, was a title of a movie, depicting and exaggerating the area for which I spent my formable years. Fort Apache historically is referred to as the "Battle of Fort Apache", whereupon the United States cavalry fought against various Apache nations and as a result the Apaches eventually were forced to move to reservations. My understanding as to why the area I grew up in was called

Fort Apache is because it looked like a war zone. This was a place where the police (mostly Caucasian which symbolized the US Calvary) were often at war with people of color (mostly Blacks and Latinos which symbolized the Apache natives) that lived in the community.

Communities like St. Mary's, contrary to its depiction in the movie *Fort Apache*, consist of hard-working people, people of color trying their best to raise their families in a safe environment. Did anyone famous come out of St. Mary's projects?

The answer depends upon your definition of famous. If famous means becoming a productive part of society without going to jail or being strung out on drugs, then the answer is yes. If your definition of famous is one who used to sell drugs and is still alive to talk about how selling drugs is wrong, then the answer is yes. St Mary's is not the home of J.B. Smooth, Jennifer Lopez, Chris Rock or any other rags to riches stories; but St Mary's did produce people that became a productive part of American mainstream society despite adversity.

These housing projects, which are now politically termed "NYCHA Housing" (New York City Housing Authority), are considered a Ghetto. A ghetto is defined as a part of a city, especially a slum area, occupied by a minority group or groups. What classified St. Mary's as a ghetto is not the people living in the projects but rather the fact that St. Mary's as well as many other projects were/are underserved in all capacities, such as capital improvements, waste removal and safety. St. Mary's consists of the poor to working poor folks for whom I always will have a special love.

This is important in context with *Cardiac Arrest* in that there is a correlation between victims of UNLAWFUL POLICE STOPS/EXCESSIVE FORCE and their socioeconomic status. It is my belief that the lower you are on the socioeconomic ladder the higher the probability that you will be a victim of an UNLAWFUL POLICE STOP or EXCESSIVE FORCE. The quote "If you can make it in New York, you can make it anywhere" was/ is appropriate if you survived growing up in the projects. Overcoming obstacles such as poverty, drugs and random violence to achieve a brighter future, which seemed to be a distant dream, did not include staying out of the cross hairs of police misconduct. Times were tough in St. Mary's, but it made for a great testing ground as to how one would manage the stressors of life, i.e. losing a job, death of a loved one or financial issues, and overcoming life's challenges.

Notwithstanding the aforementioned, as a backdrop, St. Mary's never prepared me for an UNLAWFUL POICE STOP. I was unprepared particularly because it did not occur because we had community policing and the police only detained the bad guys exclusively. Community policing was exactly that, police in your community. We had the same officers day after day, week after week, month after month, and year after year. This consistency allowed the officers policing the community to get to know the community in which they served. Over the decades it appears as if law enforcement agencies have moved away from community policing, thus being unfamiliar with the people in the community, resulting in random UNLAWFUL POLICE STOPS. Random UNLAWFUL

POLICE STOPS have become more widely acceptable and part of the fabric of life. Random UNLAWFUL POLICE STOPS have become the norm because we, people of color, have allowed this erosion of our civil rights to occur. We have allowed the erosion of our freedom from unlawful searches and seizures of our person and property. The hopeful news is that NYPD is currently working to bring back community policing and a variety of advocacy organizations, like Communities United for Police Reform (CPR), are leading the way to new legislation such as the 2018 Right to Know Act.

I must admit that back in the seventies and early eighties I was not as aware as I am now of police misconduct. My only focus was playing basketball and I was not "WOKE" to police misconduct. As a matter of fact, I don't think any of us were "WOKE". Back then police seemed to be focused on those who were doing wrong such as selling drugs, doing drugs, fighting, looking for fights, stealing or involved in gang activity. The police did not bother the working folks and working folks cooperated with the police if called upon. Presently, some police do not distinguish the good people in the community from those who want to harm the community. Policing has gone from community policing to occupying policing. Occupying policing is exactly that, where police just occupy a geographical area without any relationship to the community.

Now it seems it does not matter whether you are selling drugs or not, working or not, you will have an unfortunate UNLAWFUL POLICE STOP. I am referring to an encounter with the police that is unwarranted; where you feel harassed and where you feel like you are a criminal even though you know you did not do anything wrong criminally or otherwise. This encounter will affect you as well as other people you do not even know. This unlawful encounter may determine what profession you choose or recommend your children to consider. The consequences and ramifications of the misconduct experienced is significant in that it can influence whether the community chooses to assist the police in doing their job, which is to protect the community, or even participate in the criminal justice system such as being a juror.

The UNLAWFUL POLICE STOP will leave you wondering whether the police know you are one of the hard working, law abiding people in your community versus a criminal. Moreover, it is you that actually pay their salaries; you have rights as a person and you are conscious that the police are overstepping their boundaries by the way of their unlawful and unprofessional misconduct, thereby violating your Constitutional Rights.

Although many media outlets, from TV to social media, focus on the UNLAWFUL POLICE STOP and EXCESSIVE FORCE of African American males, the thought that only young black teenagers are unlawfully detained exclusively is false.

Anyone and everyone is prey from:

- Black and Latino;
- Young and Old;
- Males and Females;
- Immigrants;
- Rich and Poor people of color.

The word "Victim" may seem strong, but if you are a subject of an UNLAWFUL POLICE STOP, you are a victim. A victim is a person who suffers from a destructive or injurious action. Clearly, being subjected to EXCESSIVE FORCE or an UNLAWFUL POLICE STOP classifies you as a victim, whether you see it that way or not. However, as most victims of a crime, you are not to blame for this abuse of power; but, you are to blame if you are not prepared to handle the encounter.

Hopefully you will find this book helpful and unfortunately true and reflective of your experience or a familiar experience. If not, you will surely be educated at the conclusion of this book. The many missions of this book are to serve as a guide to help you handle an UNLAWFUL POLICE ENCOUNTER, understand the place from which it is derived and hopefully, just hopefully, keep you engaged in the criminal justice system and legislative process to create change.

CHAPTER 1

"KNOW YOUR AUDIENCE"

It was about 5:45 p.m. EST in December. If you are from the east coast, then you know it is dark already. On this particular evening, Black and Rick were standing in front of their building. They lived in a housing complex consisting of five, five story buildings diagrammed in a circle, with two entrances for cars to enter and exit on each side of the circle.

Rick and Black stood in front of the building; Rick smoked a cigarette while Black dribbled a basketball and occasionally threw it up against the building's brick wall. The brothers were talking about hoops when two police officers approached. Rick explained to me, as I sat in my office, how the officers approached. One officer was on his cell phone arguing with a caller as he approached Rick and Black. His partner was staring at Rick and Black with his hand on his mace spray container. Rick in his infinite wisdom muttered to himself . . .

"Here comes the bullshit."

Officer John Doe then ordered the two to clear the front of the building. Black tried to tell the officers that he and his brother lived there, although Rick did not have his identification, but the officers did not care.

Officer Jim Doe said,

"Shut the f...k up."

Black continued to bounce his basketball, which Officer John Doe grabbed and then threw the ball. Rick then motioned to go after the ball but was ordered not to move.

Black then asked,

"Why are you harassing us when we have not done anything wrong?"

At that time, a resident or two entered and exited the building greeting Rick and Black by their names each time. The officers never asked for identification to verify that Rick or Black lived in the building or to acknowledge that the young men must reside in the building because they said hello to residents that entered and exited the building of which they stood in front. The teenagers were issued a summons/ticket for trespassing.

As we sat in my office discussing their unlawful police encounter, the young teenagers became angered. Rick paced in my office, standing about 6 feet 3 inches tall, while Black, standing 6 feet 4 inches tall, joined him as they were both shaking their heads about the fact that what had occurred was not right. They were both clean shaven and physically fit. Unfortunately, they fit the stereotype of the feared "big black man" even though they did nothing wrong. Nonetheless, they were issued a summons/ticket for trespassing. Although they physically stood tall, that experience diminished their civil rights. Based on these facts, the officers did not have the right to force these men to leave the front of the building. No criminal activity occurred or appeared to be forthcoming.

Before we can discuss how to deal with this "UNLAWFUL POLICE STOP", you first must **KNOW YOUR AUDIENCE!** You must understand that police are people, too. If they have had a bad morning, or are dealing with a rough personal situation, then those emotions will not go away by the time they encounter you. If the officer(s) are frustrated, angered or dealing with a multitude of emotions, then those emotions will be present when they encounter you. Even if they suppress their emotions just prior or during their working shift does not mean said emotions are not acted out. I believe there is often a transfer of emotions in conjunction with arrogance, power issues and a lack of training and discipline that contribute to the unprofessional and UNLAWFUL POLICE STOP.

The saying "don't kick the dog because you are angry" is an appropriate adage when describing part of the UNLAWFUL POLICE STOP dynamic. I hate to say this in this way, but people of color are like the "dogs" that get kicked in these situations. Any negative/hostile energy that the officers had prior to the UNLAWFUL POLICE

STOP will more than likely be transferred to you. Police officers are people, too, and thus probably find it difficult to de-compartmentalize their emotions while on the job.

KNOW YOUR AUDIENCE is a term that politicians, lawyers, salespeople and public speakers adhere to as a rule of thumb. In business, you need to know your audience so that you can be effective in addressing your client's wants, concerns, issues and needs. For the aforementioned, it means to know to whom you are speaking, but for the contents of this book, it means to know who you are dealing with. In the situation of an UNLAWFUL POLICE STOP, the ability to size-up who you are dealing with is of utmost importance. This phrase KNOW YOUR AUDIENCE is necessary to effectively manage an UNLAWFUL POLICE STOP. Basically, it means to know who you are talking to or dealing with when you are involved in a police encounter.

So, who is your *"Audience"*?

Police officers are people like you and me, who hold prejudices, stereotypes and cultural biases as well as have personal flaws. In addition, they are often not a part of your community, in that they do not reside in your community or did not grow up in your community. Most police officers that patrol large urban/inner city/ghetto/ hood areas, or whatever term you want to use, are probably not your high school classmates and rarely are they your "peeps" from the hood. In my experience, in places like New York, most officers are not from the particular block/ neighborhood they patrol. As of 2014, it has been reported that on average among the 75 U.S. cities with the largest police force 60% of the police officers reside outside the city limits. In Los Angeles 23%, 12% in Washington, and 7% in Miami live in the city they police or in the District, as to Washington exclusively, based on statistics from the articles "Most Police Don't Live in the City They Serve", August 20, 2014, and "Should NYPD Officers Be Required to Live in NYC", August 21, 2014.

I suspect the above respective percentages will only decrease given most police benevolent associations are against any residency requirements. On the other end of the spectrum, African American and Latino officers, 80% and 75% respectively, live in the above-mentioned boroughs; however, given they are a minority within most police departments makes this a moot point.

The NYC Police Benevolent Association has argued, in the past, that it is too expensive for officers to live in the five boroughs (Bronx, Brooklyn, Queens, Manhattan and Staten Island). This argument is flawed because there are countless of New York State/City employees with comparable salaries or less residing in the Bronx, Brooklyn, Queens and Manhattan. It is my belief that a residency requirement in large cities like New York would create a community policing environment and thereby reduce the number of lawsuits filed stemming from UNLAWFUL POLICE STOPS and EXCESSIVE FORCE. A residency requirement should be appealing to police officers who view their profession as a career. Additionally, the City should see it as appealing for financial reasons, jury financial awards/financial settlements, and the communities serviced to ensure safety. The residency requirement could be waived after a certain number of years on the police force or for an officer that had resided in the five boroughs their entire life prior to becoming a police officer. Without a residency requirement, you are left with police who do not live in your community and therefore do not know anything about your community or have a vested interest in the community they are trying to serve. This is our current state of policing and it is proving to be unsuccessful.

Getting to know your *"Audience"*

Having had the experience of working with the police, as a prosecutor and defense attorney, ensuring the accused's civil rights are not violated by them, I have learned that some police officers are conditioned to taking orders and giving orders. They are trained as if they are soldiers in the military. Some will say rightfully so given the totality of the job, but I disagree. Typically, police officers that abuse their power often do not want to be questioned by civilians and view being questioned as a threat or insubordination of some sort. Questioning an officer is not received well let alone questioning an abusive officer. Questioning orders given by police is disturbing to the abusive officer and your questions are viewed as an imminent threat, which can result in verbal and physical abuse. The police commissioner typically gives orders, like in New York, and those orders are communicated all the way down to the local/precinct cop who serves your community. The local police then give orders to the community they patrol to execute the Commissioner's order. An example is the de facto (unwritten policy) quota system officers must follow such as issuing "X" number of summons/tickets monthly. If an officer does not meet this quota of summons/tickets, then it is quite possible future promotions will not occur. In one case, twelve New York

City police officers (NYPD 12) are suing the NYCPD for enforcing a "quota system" and retaliating against them by not promoting them or transferring said officers to remote locations for not enforcing said "quota system". See The New Yorker article "A NYPD SERGEANT BLOWS THE WHISTLE ON QUOTAS", August 27, 2018.

In most police encounters, the police give countless orders. Search your brain and ask yourself what was the first thing Officer John Doe said to you when he stopped you while you were driving. What did the Cop say to you when he/she approached your vehicle?

"LICENSE AND REGISTRATION" *(an order)*

"KEEP YOUR HANDS WHERE I CAN SEE THEM." (an order)

If you're ordered to exit said vehicle:
"STAND THERE"
and possibly
"SHUT UP",
if you question the stop (an order)

If you are walking and you are stopped by a police officer, what is the first thing the Officer says?
"LET ME SEE SOME ID!" (an order)

All of the above statements are orders. There is very little, if any, conversation between the civilian and the detaining officer. Understanding your audience is critical in how you handle yourself and manage the situation. If a police officer is told he/she needs to issue "X" amount of tickets this month, then you can bet come hell or high water, whether right or wrong, he/she will reach that number "X". Thus, if the officers who UNLAWFULLY detained Rick and Black were under orders to issue "X" number of summons/tickets to meet a de facto quota system, it is irrelevant whether Rick and/or Black had not committed a crime. Pursuant to a de facto quota system, a summons/ ticket for trespassing would be issued. If a police officer is told to arrest all African American males between the ages of 18-25 whose pants are hanging low below their waist, then you better believe if you fit that description you will be issued a summons or arrested. This is notwithstanding the fact there is nothing criminal about dressing in a particular style.

In the case of Rick/Black's scenario, it can be argued that these officers were blindly adhering to the orders of his/her commanding officer. These officers were following their chain of command; they were ordered to reach a quota as to issuing summons or making arrests. Irrespective of criminality, they would reach that quota at the expense of Rick and Black. Knowing your audience is critical to managing the UNLAWFUL ENCOUNTER. Rick and Black's scenario reveals one group of police that, for purposes of this guide, I will name QUOTA COPS. Described below are a few definitions I have created for these classifications of the various "audiences" you might encounter when dealing with police. Additionally, these classifications are not a blanket description of all police officers, just those who abuse the civil rights of law-abiding citizens.

QUOTA COP - an officer that makes decisions, UNLAWFUL STOPS and arrests to satisfy a de facto quota system.

PREJUDICED COP - an officer that makes decisions, UNLAWFUL STOPS, and arrests based solely on race, ethnic and cultural bias.

CLASSIST COP - an officer who makes decisions, UNLAWFUL STOPS, and arrests grounded on envy, given the detained civilian appears to be of the upper middle class to upper class and the CLASSIST COP also has disdain for poor people of color because he/she believes they have no rights.

POWER COP - an officer that abuses his/her authority professionally and physically, to the disadvantage of others, in conducting an UNLAWFUL STOP or using EXCESSIVE FORCE. Statistics show a disproportionate number of those who encounter POWER COPS are people of color and those who are economically disadvantaged.

While these are broad categories, all categories of cops have a common thread. These groups of officers will give orders during your encounter and will not tolerate any conversation and more importantly questions. These are the types of officers you may encounter during an UNLAWFUL POLICE STOP. Any analysis of UNLAWFUL POLICE

STOPS or EXCESSIVE FORCE issues viewed from purely a racial perspective would not be complete. The BLACK vs. WHITE analysis only scratches the surface of the bigger problem, although people of color are the most victimized. I suspect a more in-depth analysis would reveal that it is less about Black and White but more about officers vs. civilians and the power struggle that occurs when an order is questioned or when a police officer is questioned in most cases.

If we reflect on Rick's and Black's UNLAWFUL STOP pursuant to a Quota Cop detention, it would not have mattered whether Rick or Black lived in the building in front of which they stood; they both were going to be issued a summons/ tickets. The ethnicity or race of the offending officers was irrelevant; Rick and Black were still going to receive a summons or be arrested because a quota had to be met. With this understanding, comments regarding volunteering identification or information to support the premise that they were not trespassing would not have saved these teenagers from the UNLAWFUL STOP and false summons/arrest.

TACTICAL DO'S AND DON'TS TO REMEMBER:
DO'S

1. Always have identification. In Rick's and Black's case, Rick had no ID, so he couldn't have even tried to convince the detaining officers not to issue a summons/ticket.

2. Use your **"smart phone"** wisely and stop using it exclusively for social media purposes. Use your phone to take and save a picture of your Government Issued ID, in case you find you have lost or left it at home during the time of your UNLAWFUL POLICE STOP. This will ensure you have some form of ID on you at all times.

3. Know you have the right to ask why you are being detained or arrested. Be aware that there is no civil rights or criminal violation if the detaining officer does not respond.

4. Always recruit bystanders as witnesses. Rick and Black should have asked the residents they spoke to entering and exiting the building to stay present or to verify that the two lived in the building.

5. Know there is no law that requires you to have identification and you can refuse to provide ID. Police can never compel you to produce ID unless they have reasonable suspicion to believe you are involved in illegal activity.

DON'TS

1. Do not aggravate the UNLAWFUL STOP by arguing with the detaining cop if you see him/her already aggravated while approaching or if you observe an officer with his/her hands

on their mace while approaching, i.e. Rick muttering "Here comes the bullshit"; Black asking "Why are we being harassed?" and continuing to dribble while the officers are drafting the summons/tickets.

2. Do not make any sudden movements, i.e. Black motioning to retrieve the ball thrown by the officer. This could be perceived as resisting arrest, like running away during the detention.

CHAPTER 2

I DIDN'T DO "NUFFIN"!

Whether you are a kid from the projects (was that), an up and coming professional (doing that), or a distinguished elder of the African American Community (hope to become that), at some point in your life you or someone you are close to will likely encounter an UNLAWFUL POLICE STOP. According to Jesper Ryberg's (2011) article "Racial Profiling and Criminal Justice" published in the Journal of Ethics, racial profiling exists and, as a practical matter, it is reflected in the detention of people of color. Moreover, African Americans and Latinos generally represent more than 85% of those stopped by police, though their combined population make up a small share of the city's racial composition as seen in New York City.

A study consisting of statistics from the Center for Disease Control and Prevention, FBI, state police websites, hospital records and two investigative series by the Washington Post and Guardian newspapers reveal Blacks and Native Americans had the highest stop/arrest rates per 10,000 population than Whites-non-Hispanics and Asians as of July 25, 2016. Rates are important because they account for each group's proportion of the population. Blacks make up about 13% of the US population but account for 28% of arrests.

It is highly likely you or someone you know will be unlawfully stopped by the police; therefore, it is critical you recognize when it is happening and how to manage the UNLAWFUL POLICE STOP from the beginning to the end and not let it manage you.

This may sound like common sense, but I have come to learn sometimes sense is not so common. An analysis of the detention of "Bi-Fo" can hopefully illustrate how an UNLAWFUL POLICE STOP occurs and ways to manage the unlawful detention.

During the interview of witnesses to Bi-Fo's (short for bifocals) UNLAWFUL STOP, they explained what they witnessed as they crossed the street to watch.

Bi-Fo asked why he was being stopped, asserted that he did not have to show ID, and told the officer not to touch him and to get her hands out of his pockets.

The female officer, Jane Doe, responded that she could stop him if she wanted and demanded to see Bi-Fo's ID. Officer Jane Doe further exclaimed that she was only going to tell him one time, then added sarcastically, *"You should be upstairs anyway on a school night."*

Bi-Fo replied, *"You're tripping, I'm coming from basketball practice and I have no curfew"*, as he was slammed against a fence with his sweat pants and shorts hanging so below his waist you could see his underwear. Bi-Fo went on to say, *"You don't know me; I'm in prep school and bustin' straight B's."*

Officer Jane Doe replied by saying, *"I don't need to know you. You need to know me and show me some respect."*

Bi-Fo then pulled out his cell phone and attempted to call his parents, as a crowd formed inclusive of the two witnesses. The crowd was heated and very expressive as they yelled "Why are you arresting him" and shouted, "Stop harassing him", among other things. To no avail Bi-Fo was arrested on the spot, subsequent to a search and the smashing of his cell phone. Bi-Fo was falsely charged with disorderly conduct although his conduct was not criminal or disorderly. Bi-Fo broke no laws. If I had to characterize what category these group of police officers belong to, given the facts in this scenario, then I would say they were PREDJUDICE COPS. PREDJUDICE COPS are officers that make decisions and arrests solely on race, ethnic and cultural bias. Bi-Fo was the subject of that abuse of power. Based on the facts, as narrated by the witnesses, Bi-Fo did nothing wrong criminally or otherwise. His conduct was not disorderly; he had the right to ask a question; he had the right to refuse to be searched and give identification. The exchange between Bi-Fo and the detaining officers was more about what the officers could or could not do and less about whether Bi-Fo actually committed a crime. **Bi-Fo was stopped because he was a young Black teenager dressed a certain way and presumed to be up to no good.**

As I reflect on my formative years, folks in St. Mary's Projects were stopped all the time. I assumed then it was because they did something wrong as I watched those who were detained just brush it off. Bi-Fo and his witnesses displayed the same brush-off attitude I have seen in the past as if the UNLAWFUL POLICE STOP was the normal way of life. Bi-Fo's UNLAWFUL STOP may be the norm for many but it should not be.

In review, Bi-Fo thought that by informing the officers that he was a prep school student with good grades and coming from basketball practice he would have altered the chain of events. This information did not change the UNLAWFUL STOP, police harassment, illegal search and false arrest. These officers did not care about Bi-Fo's background or his future trajectory. Bi-Fo's pedigree did not matter.

PLEASE BE ADVISED: *You will never be able to prevent an UNLAWFUL POLICE STOP from occurring no matter what you say, and it is most likely what you say will only incur an unfavorable response like "I do not care or shut up.".*

Remember your audience:

- QUOTA COP
- PREJUDICED COP
- CLASSIST COP
- POWER COP

Blacks and Native Americans between the ages of 15-29 have the highest arrest rate per 10,000 populations; this is inclusive of arrests stemming from UNLAWFUL POLICE STOPS. The young and poor incur the highest number of UNLAWFUL POLICE STOPS and most police misconduct incidents suffered by the young and poor are not traceable because no complaint was ever filed. I suspect the lack of faith in the police department disciplining their own for misconduct; the fear of repercussions and the ugly truth that for some this is a way of life. Furthermore, if underserved or over-policed communities complain, no one would listen, as the evidence would show from protests that highlight these issues. This creates a vicious cycle whereupon the police are empowered to continue racial profiling as well as other illegal conduct-misconduct. For example, the NYCLU (New York Civil Liberties Union) revealed that New Yorkers have been subject to police stops and police interrogations for more than 5 million times since 2002. More importantly, Black/Latino communities continue to be the overwhelming target of these tactics, for which nearly 9 out of 10 "stop & frisk" New Yorkers have been completely innocent.

I remember when my best friend Teddy Black would say "I can't wait till we get older, so we won't have to go through this bullshit!" At that time, we were in our teens, young and poor. We thought the older we became the less UNLAWFUL STOPS we would encounter. Off to college we went, and after successfully graduating, we were still victims of UNLAWFUL POLICE STOPS. Even after we entered Professional schools, "Graduate" and "Law" school, respectively, we still said, "Can't wait until we graduate so we won't have to go through this bullshit." The sad reality is that you cannot run away or prevent an UNLAWFUL POLICE STOP. You cannot prevent it from occurring because you do not control when or where it happens; there is no expiration date.

My life experiences led me to believe the more financial wealth you obtain and the quicker you relocate to the suburbs or a gated community the UNLAWFUL POLICE STOPS decline. Decline but DO NOT GO AWAY. The idea that you have made it in society, that you have arrived and are protected from an UNLAWFUL POLICE STOP, creates a false sense of security. Just ask Jeff Blake, African American US tennis star, NBA player Theo Sefolosha and Harvard Professor Henry Louis Gates Wells; they all are financially secure and by most standards made it in America but yet were subjected to an UNLAWFUL POLICE STOP.

One should understand an UNLAWFUL POLICE STOP can occur notwithstanding your socioeconomic status in life and thus you should always be prepared. In our previous story about Bi-Fo, he was not prepared and ill-equipped to manage this encounter. Bi-Fo's attempt to call his parents failed because he announced his intentions. Moreover, Bi-Fo did not have an alternative plan such as yelling his parents' telephone number to the onlooking crowd and then pleading for someone to call his parents after the police smashed his cell phone. Bi-Fo did not have a multi-level plan to manage his unlawful detention.

TACTICAL DO'S AND DON'TS TO REMEMBER:

DO'S

1. Inform the officers you do not consent to any search of your person or property.

2. Repeat to the detaining officers that any search is non-consensual to bystanders.

3. Reveal that you do not have ID if in fact you do not have ID; be honest (*always carry your ID/smart phone).

4. Know in most states it is not a crime not to have ID.

5. Have your cell phone accessible, not in a bag or in your pocket but rather in your hands; use speech/voice dial to make a call.

6. Just call; do not announce who you are calling.

7. Solicit the crowd or bystanders to help by having them video or call a contact, hopefully family.

DON'TS

1. Do not physically try to stop a police officer from illegally searching you because it will always lead to physical abuse/EXCESSIVE FORCE.

2. Do not reach into your pockets or bags if stopped without loudly verbalizing to the world to hear what you are retrieving , i.e. smart phone.

3. Do not argue with the detaining officers especially when they are being aggressive, hostile, rude, sarcastic or condescending.

4. Do not announce who you intend to call; just call.

5. Do not try to convince the police you are a good person because it will likely fall on deaf ears and possibly irritate the detaining officers.

CHAPTER 3

WE ASK THE QUESTIONS!

"E", a thirty-two-year-old Latino male, was visiting his girlfriend (girl) in the projects. He did not have a key to get into the building and the intercom/buzzer system was busted. "E" called his girl on her cell phone and asked her to come down to let him into the building. She responded, "Are you kidding, wait for someone to leave the building and then enter". "E" settled for that answer and waited. As he waited, two officers noticed him standing outside the building. The two officers approached him as he waited and asked where he was going. "E" informed them he was going to visit his girlfriend and stated: "What's with the questions?"

> *The officers replied, "We do the questioning – ya hear!"*

This is when the questioning really started flowing. The police began to bombard him with questions demanding to know his complete name, his age, his girl's apartment number, the length of the relationship, his possession of weapons on his person, and finally if they could search him and if they searched him would they find any illegal contraband.

"E" chose not to answer their questions. During this time, his girl started blowing up his cell. He wanted to reach for his cell in his back pocket but was fearful of retrieving his phone because he was scared that he may be shot if he reached. He alerted the cops he wanted to retrieve his cell, which is smart preventing any misunderstanding, but the officers did not respond. "E" retrieved his phone given no response and asked his girl to come downstairs to verify he was visiting her. However, by the time she made it downstairs, "E" was already being handcuffed. "E's" girlfriend followed behind him as she yelled at the cops: "He was not doing nuffin!" "E" was escorted to the police vehicle, placed inside and arrested.

In this scenario "E" was not required to give his entire pedigree but just established he was not loitering/ trespassing. Loitering is defined as standing or waiting around idly or without apparent purpose. Trespassing is defined as entering onto property without permission. "E" explained to me he felt disrespected when questioned by the police; he was not required to divulge any information about who he was visiting to establish he was not loitering or trespassing. As a result of his state of annoyance, "E" did not assess what type of police officer he was dealing with to have an understanding that the information he refused to provide would lead to his arrest. Having an understanding as to the type of officer one could encounter (QUOTA, PREJUDICED, CLASSIST or POWER COP) and having the ability to take that information into consideration when managing the UNLAWFUL POLICE STOP would have served to "E's" benefit.

Although "E" was just standing waiting for an opportunity to enter the building to visit his girlfriend, he could be considered loitering or trespassing. The conventional belief "I can stand anywhere; this is America" is not always true. For instance, in New York the local precincts have partnerships with numerous residential buildings that allow the police to inquire whether a person lives in the residence or is visiting someone in the residence when they see a person standing in front of the building for an extended period of time. The question is who determines what an extended period of time is. In my experience, you know it when you see it. Thus, refusing to answer questions in this scenario could be more harmful than helpful and could possibly escalate matters.

Moreover, being annoyed, feeling disrespected and humiliated prevented "E" from getting the critical information necessary to file a complaint or commence a lawsuit for false arrest. Said critical information includes:

- The officers' names
- The officers' shield number
- The Precinct
- The "Routine Motor Patrol Car" (RMP)/Police Car license plate

"E's" girlfriend also missed this same opportunity as she screamed about being disrespected because one of the officers told her to "Mind your business before you're arrested!" as "E" was placed into an RMP. All parties involved in an UNLAWFUL POLICE STOP must be prepared to retrieve the information necessary to be able to seek future redress like file a complaint against the offending officer. You must always remember police, in their mind, do not need a reason to stop you, so stop expecting a logical answer when you ask, "Why are you stopping me?" This question will only serve to frustrate you because the given answer will mostly likely be contrived. The offending officer, on the other hand, then becomes hostile and the level of annoyance increases for all parties involved. Explaining to the offending officers that, "You didn't do nuffin" will not prevent the UNLAWFUL POLICE STOP from occurring.

Understanding you do not control when the UNLAWFUL POLICE STOP will occur is part of being mentally prepared because it will hopefully allow you to focus on some of the critical information warranted to seek redress like in the 2018 Collar for Dollar Lawsuit, where it is alleged that a false arrest case was routinely conducted near the end of the shift for cops to pocket extra overtime pay. Once again, retrieving critical information is in your control and not how long you will be unlawfully detained. Managing your emotions is in your control and not the fact you have been a victim of an UNLAWFUL POLICE STOP and the length of your detention.

As a kid from the Bronx walking across the Willis Ave Bridge and the 145th Street Bridge to and from Harlem, not once did I think being stopped by the police was in my best interest. It was not like the cops were detaining me to inquire whether I was going to commit suicide by jumping off one of those bridges. The unlawful detention was not to seek information as to a crime but rather to harass a young black male. As I reflect on being illegally stopped,

I thought it was a part of life, nothing unusual. Then and now I realize explaining to the detaining officers that I am not doing "nuffin" would have not made a difference; the UNLAWFUL POLICE STOP would have occurred regardless. My not doing "nuffin" wrong did not prevent or shorten the UNLAWFUL POLICE STOP and neither will your volunteered explanation.

Whether you are unlawfully detained by a QUOTA COP, a PREJUDICED COP, a CLASSIST COP or a POWER COP, it does not matter whether you were doing "nuffin" wrong at the time of your detention; looking for a rational reason as to why you were being unlawfully detained is useless.

Understanding the above is preparing yourself mentally and emotionally to manage the UNLAWFUL POLICE STOP in a manner that you can retrieve the critical information to file a complaint or commence a lawsuit for false arrest in the future.

TACTICAL DO'S AND DON'TS TO REMEMBER:
DO'S

1. Answer the officers' questions if it is relevant to the circumstances. Such as in "E's" case, give the appropriate information pertaining to exactly where your girlfriend lives only. As a matter of fact, have the officers call her in your presence.

2. Look at the officer's badge for his name or shield and contain your emotions of feeling disrespected, annoyed and humiliated.

3. Retain the police vehicle license plates if the detaining officer's shield and badge is not visible.

4. Understand for every action there is a reaction; so by refusing to answer appropriate questions, the reaction could lead to a hostile environment and more importantly your arrest.

5. Recognize that volunteering information that supports your non-criminal activity may not resolve the UNLAWFUL STOP, thus being annoyed as well as other emotions may prevent you from retrieving critical information.

6. Ask if you can retrieve your cell phone or any other item on your person.

7. Announce out loud that you are retrieving the item and confirm that the officers approved this action.

DON'TS

1. Do not volunteer information that is not necessary.

2. Do not argue with the detaining officer.

3. Do not let your emotions of feeling disrespected, annoyed or humiliated prevent you from retrieving critical information like name, shield number of the detaining officer(s) and the car license plate of the police car.

4. Do not let others involved fail you by not retrieving the information that is critical to filing a complaint about the UNLAWFUL STOP. In "E's" case, instead of screaming at the officers, his girlfriend should have been retrieving the warranted information to assist "E" in the future.

5. Do not reach for anything on your person or into a bag without the police giving a verbal consent of "Yes" or "No".

6. Do not reach for an item on your person if the officers are non-responsive to your request.

CHAPTER 4

BE AWARE!

As I drove from the South Orange train station, the ritzier part of Essex County in New Jersey, I observed in my rear-view mirror a police car with its top lights flashing as well as flashing headlights speeding behind me. At first, I thought nothing of the police car speeding some distance behind me; therefore, I continued my phone conversation. To me, it was just a police car rushing to a potential emergency. I said to myself, "I know they are not chasing me," but then I quickly realized that I was a black male in a 350 Lexus driving through an exclusive part of town at night. I then immediately drove over to the right side of the road to see if they wanted to pass but that was wishful thinking; I was pulled over. I alerted my caller to act as an active listener, third party witness. My cell was placed on my console attached to a stand-alone cell phone holder. Thus, I was not concerned with having to retrieve it giving the impression that I was concealing anything illegal or receiving a ticket for talking on the phone while driving. I did turn off the screen to ensure the detaining officers did not know I had a third-party ear witness.

The African American officer approached my driver's side window with one hand on his holster and the other hand on his shining flashlight as . . . order, after order, after order, after order . . . occurred to which I complied retrieving all paperwork requested. During this time, his partner stood at the rear passenger side of my car. The officer, later to be identified as Officer Johnson, took my driver's license and went to his car, I assume to check my identity among other things. Officer Johnson eventually returned and I asked, "Is everything alright, Officer Johnson?", making sure to state his name. I was then rudely told to be careful and to drive off.

Just prior to the stop, I was on my speakerphone and I informed the caller of what was about to happen. I wanted the caller to be an ear witness to the UNLAWFUL POLICE "CAR" STOP. I believe the stop was unlawful because it appeared it was just to check my identity to see if I lived in the area or to check to see if I had any warrants. The detention/stop was not based on me speeding, driving with a suspended license, or playing loud music. I was not given a warning or told I was tailgating, had a broken taillight, or was using my cell phone improperly. This was a case of Driving While Black (DWB).

In the article "The Big Question about Why Police Pull Over So Many Black Drivers", July 8, 2016, President Obama recounts how he was stopped while driving for no reason except Driving While Black (DWB). Obama publicly stated, ". . . there are a lot of African Americans-not just me who have that same kind of story being pulled over . . ." Moreover, data shows that this is not aberration. The fact that Blacks get pulled over on the road more than Whites has been a fact of American life. The article cited above further articulated the pervasiveness of racial profiling by law enforcement is grounded in our Nation's drug laws, which escalated car stops among people of color, notwithstanding that drug use or trafficking is not confined to racial and ethnic minorities in the U.S. Nonetheless, the war on drugs has targeted people of color and has become a proxy for criminality. See "Driving While Black: Racial Profiling on our Nation's Highways", June 1999. Law enforcement agencies have argued that making disproportionate numbers of traffic stops among African Americans and other minorities is not discrimination but rational law enforcement. Data on driver's race in police records is sparse and it is hard to capture what is happening on a national scale as it relates to racial profiling and traffic stops. However, it is safe to say African Americans are detained at a higher rate, are given more tickets when detained, are arrested more often for driving on a suspended license, or unpaid ticket, and are more likely to be subjected to a vehicle search or EXCESSIVE FORCE than Whites. Notwithstanding the suggested data, in my scenario I was not detained or cited for some traffic infraction or based on the assumption I was trafficking illegal contraband. I was stopped because I was Driving While Black (DWB).

I would categorize my detaining officer as a CLASSIST COP. As previously defined, a CLASSIST COP is a police officer who is envious of your material property such as your car and is annoyed that he/she would have to work twice as hard to purchase your vehicle. This emotion is played out in their work by way of an UNLAWFUL STOP. Remember, police are people, too, who have feelings and frustrations that are not always de-compartmentalized while they perform their job, which is to protect and serve.

It should be noted at the time of the stop I did not think it was racially motivated because Officer Johnson was African American. Thinking in retrospect, this was a narrow point of view given the studies on implicit bias that exist within one's own culture. Implicit bias is an unconscious thought concerning particular qualities one assigns to a certain social group.

As I stated previously, just prior to the stop, I was on my speakerphone and I informed the caller of what was about to happen. I wanted the caller to be an ear witness to the UNLAWFUL POLICE STOP. Establishing an independent witness is vital when you are alone and you encounter an UNLAWFUL POLICE STOP. You always want a third-party witness. You never just want it to be your word against the offending police officer's word because most people are subconsciously trained to believe the police.

Establishing an ear witness, in this case, helped in managing the UNLAWFUL POLICE STOP, in that I had another person that could serve as a recorder of the unfolding events. For example, by me stating the officer's last name when I asked the officer if everything was alright, I was able to ensure the ear witness could write it down allowing me to focus on other critical information. By saying "How can I help you Officer X" or "Is everything alright Officer X" loudly and clearly, the caller was able to memorialize the offending officer's last name. It is important to remember to inform the listener to be an active listener and to reframe from talking while the UNLAWFUL STOP is occurring. Establishing a witness allowed me to remain composed and focused to obtain the critical information necessary to file a complaint or lawsuit thereafter. I could focus on the shield number/badge of the offending officer and his partner's information.

As Officer Johnson went to his car, I continued to talk to my ear witness filling them in on as much information as I could. I reminded them to listen intently while I spoke with the Officer, and to copy down the information that I relayed to them. I gave them the officer's shield number as well as his partner's name and shield number to the best of my ability. I had to gather this information through my passenger mirror. By verbalizing to the listener or committing to memory the badge numbers, you can always retrace the offending police officer's name, his partner's name and the assigned precinct.

Although, in that instance, I appeared to be composed and had a plan by having an ear witness, internally I felt like I was having a heart attack. My heart was beating fast along with having sweaty hands and my blood pressure rising all because I could not control the outcome and I knew I did nothing wrong. I was infuriated because I could not totally control the situation and my civil rights were being violated. However, I did not let my emotions get the best of me and I had a plan and I worked that plan even though it felt like I was going into *Cardiac Arrest*. The first level of preparedness is "AWARENESS".

BE AWARE!

Be aware in that if you are alone and you are the subject of an UNLAWFUL POLICE STOP you should use your cell phone to call someone to serve as an ear witness to the encounter. If you suspect you are going to be UNLAWFULLY STOPPED while driving, then make the call or activate your recording device before the Officer approaches your vehicle. If you have no one to call, then solicit help from people who may be observing the encounter.

Note, in my case, I was lucky to have someone on the phone already. Also note despite being polite when I asked "Is everything alright Officer Johnson" I was still met with resistance when rudely told to be careful and to drive off.

Take notice that I did not ask the offending officers why they stopped me or ask "what's the problem officer(s)" because I knew these questions would not prevent, stop or derail the UNLAWFUL POLICE STOP. The statements or questions would be received as hostile communications.

My life experience has led me to believe asking questions when you are unlawfully detained will only be met with resistance. Also, you never want to ask for a badge/shield number, if you can avoid it. Requesting a badge number signals to an officer that a complaint will be forthcoming and that will serve to annoy the offending officer. The offending officer will most likely arrest you and fabricate a narrative to justify his misconduct and the arrest itself. Also, asking for a badge/shield number may cause the officer to conceal the badge number.

In asking questions you will mostly incur the following: no response, a hostile response, a fabrication (lie) or the lost opportunity to just observe and memorize the information necessary to file a complaint or lawsuit. Negative, hostile, angry communication or a visible display of displeasure will only attract the same communication, pushing you further away from your goal of retrieving critical information to file a complaint/lawsuit and ensuring your safety.

The purpose of filing a complaint or lawsuit, beyond personal justice, is to be able to track profiling and deter police misconduct, the UNLAWFUL STOP, as well as to receive financial compensation for trauma, pain and suffering and emotional/mental anguish you may have suffered.

Some file a complaint/lawsuit solely to be financially compensated for their trauma, pain and suffering or emotional/mental anguish. Others file a complaint/lawsuit seeking not only financial compensation but also systemic change. In this case the lawsuit/complaint serves to track certain officers or precinct's misconduct in hopes that the offending officer is terminated or the leadership within the misguided precinct is changed. The ultimate goal is to deter police misconduct in order to ensure civilian-police trust, which would restore the faith of people of color in the criminal justice system.

In my scenario things could have unraveled, leading to a longer detention, an arrest or even death, based on my life experiences. Questions such as "What's the problem officer?" or "Why did you stop me?", or saying "You know you're just harassing me," would have only served to escalate the matter although that was not the intent. Moreover, any of the above questions or statements would have again led to a hostile exchange, which could have led to an extended detention, arrest or death.

It is my belief that my questions would have not been viewed as questions or an exercise of my First Amendment Right – Freedom of Speech – but rather as challenging

Officer Johnson's authority. Life experience has revealed no one likes their authority to be challenged especially police officers. Thus, the asking of questions translates into challenging authority, which can escalate an UNLAWFUL POLICE STOP and turn the UNLAWFUL POLICE STOP into a case of EXCESSIVE FORCE. It also can lead to the illegal search of your vehicle or person as well as an arrest to justify the detention. Keeping in mind that for every action there will be a reaction should prove helpful in managing an UNLAWFUL POLICE STOP by carefully choosing what you say and how you say it to the offending officer.

As you may be aware from personal experience or from social media, a variety of car stops lead to fatalities. It is easy to fault the police given their training or lack of training when there is a fatality as a result of a car stop, but I would be remised if I did not mention as the detained person I have the obligation not to escalate the tension/UNLAWFUL STOP by way of the tone in which I exercise my First Amendment Right – Freedom of Speech – or take liberties in a situation for which I know I should not, such as spontaneously reaching into my glove compartment.

REMEMBER

- Do not verbally aggravate the situation, which could ultimately lead to your arrest or EXCESSIVE FORCE.

- Do not take liberties when you know you should not. For instance, do not exit your vehicle unless you are ordered.

- Do not tell the detaining officer what he/she can or cannot do. If you are a victim of an UNLAWFUL STOP, then what an officer can and cannot do is irrelevant.

- Do not take the liberty to reach into any pockets on your person or the glove compartment without permission and verbally announcing what you are doing and why. For instance, "Can I go into my glove compartment, Officer Johnson?" "Officer Johnson, I am now going into my glove compartment as you granted to retrieve my insurance or driver's license." This may sound extreme or extra, but this is the world we live in and the objective is to get home alive.

In some cases, you may be better off consenting to the detaining officer retrieving the requested paperwork from your glove compartment only or your head visor. This little intrusion for a person of color may help avoid a nightmare encounter or physical abuse. **You must remember from a police officer's perspective their safety is first which translates to your safety being last.**

Although, I am not a police officer, I do understand that any traffic stop is potentially dangerous because the officer does not know who he/she is approaching and cannot see everything the person is doing in the vehicle as they approach. Therefore, I understand the shining of a flashlight and having one's hand on the holster may be police protocol when executing a traffic stop. However, I also believe good policing is having the ability to consider the detained person's perspective once all safety concerns are satisfied when performing police work. Therefore, the detaining officer(s) should understand that if he/she stops a person of color and that person believes they committed no crime, then it is likely that person's perception of the detention is based on racial profiling (DWB) or the officer's desire to harass or fulfill some quota or based on classism. (CLASSIST COP). This perception in conjunction with the lack of transparency becomes reality and supports the claim for abuse of power, adhering to quotas, the theory of classism and racial profiling (DWB). Hopefully, having the above understanding will assist you in managing the stop and dictate your actions because **for every action there is a reaction**.

The first obligation I discussed previously is to not verbally aggravate the situation, which could ultimately lead to your arrest or EXCESSIVE FORCE. The second obligation is not to take liberties when you know you should not. For instance, do not exit your vehicle unless you are ordered. Another example of taking liberties is telling the detaining officer what he/she can or cannot do. It is obvious that if you are a victim of an UNLAWFUL STOP then what an officer can and cannot do is irrelevant. Most importantly, do not take the liberty to reach into any pockets on your person or the glove compartment without permission and verbally announcing what you are doing and why. For instance, "Can I go into my glove compartment, Officer Johnson?" "Officer Johnson, I am now going into my glove compartment as you order me to retrieve my insurance or driver's license." This may sound extreme or extra but, again, this is the world we live in and the objective is to get home alive.

TACTICAL DO'S AND DON'TS TO REMEMBER:

DO'S

1. Have a user-friendly driver license, **i.e. smile in your photo and dress appropriately**.

2. Call an "ear witness" prior to the police approaching your vehicle.

3. Initiate any recording devices you possess prior to the police encounter.

4. Ask permission to retrieve documentation as ordered.

5. Verbalize that you are retrieving the documents only.

6. Access who is actually detaining you (QUOTA COP, POWER COP, CLASSIST COP, PREJUDICED COP) so that you can understand what the detaining officer's trigger points are.

7. Actually think about whether asking questions or verbalizing your annoyance/irritation is appropriate given your particular circumstances.

8. Understand that "**For every Action there is a Reaction**."

9. Call for a Supervisor (if possible).

10. BE AWARE!

DON'TS

1. Do not exit your vehicle unless ordered.

2. Do not assume anything you say will be received as just an expression of your Freedom of Speech.

3. Do not reach into your pockets on your person or into your glove compartment without permission.

4. Do not argue with the detaining officer.

5. Do not show immediate annoyance, disrespect, agitation or hostility. **Hostility will only be met with more Hostility.**

6. Do not consent to the search of your entire car.

7. Do not expect a positive reaction in response to your action. **For every action there is a reaction**.

8. Do not become a lawyer or civil rights activist during your UNLAWFULL STOP. It is not

the time nor place to educate the detaining officer or showcase your knowledge of Search and Seizure 14th Amendment Constitutional Rights.

9. Do not have tints so dark on your car windows that the police cannot see into the car. Do not act like you know the tint on your windows is legal because every state has different standards.

10. Do not argue with the police that the tints on your windows are standard/legal unless you have documented proof.

11. Do not have any outstanding warrants or delinquent child support orders which will lead to your arrest.

CHAPTER 5

BE PREPARED

The Wrights sat in my office as they recounted the events that led to Don being a victim of EXCESSIVE FORCE. Don and his wife, Sade, stated that they got into an argument and things got really hot and heavy from name calling to cursing to threats of violence.

Sade relayed that she had threatened to call the police and have Don arrested. Don dared Sade to do just that and call the police. Don stated: "I wish the police would enter my apartment." Sade continued to recount that she called 911 to have Don removed from the home. Shortly thereafter, unbeknownst to Don, the police arrived banging aggressively and loudly on the apartment door. Don in his arrogant way continued to undress down to his boxers. Meanwhile, Sade ran to the door and let the police into the apartment as she explained she wanted Don out.

Don heard the commotion and "sauntered" slowly down the stairs and said to the officers "What's the problem?" Immediately, Don was battered, assaulted and placed in handcuffs. As a result of the officer's EXCESSIVE FORCE/misconduct, Don suffered a fractured eye socket while he yelled, "You can't arrest me in my own apartment; you need an arrest warrant!"

Don was mistaken because Sade had called the police and consented to their entrance. Sade, on the other hand, only wanted Don to leave the apartment and was not prepared for the officers' EXCESSIVE FORCE response or Don's arrest. Don thought he knew his rights but he did not, and Sade thought she could control the outcome once the police arrived but she was not prepared.

A 911 call to the police for assistance involving Domestic Violence will always result in one of the parties of the residence being ordered to leave. The minimal result of a call for Domestic Violence is one party leaving the home; however, it often leads to an arrest. When responding to a 911 domestic violence call, police cannot take the risk of allowing the parties to resolve their differences alone. Thus, the parties' (Sade and Don) family unit will be broken for fear that physical abuse, further physical abuse or a fatality may occur due to the officer's failure to protect and serve. However, protect and serve does not mean you are subjected to EXCESSIVE FORCE, like Don.

The POWER COP in Don and Sade's scenario used his power to abuse Don for whatever reason. That reason may be because he/she does not like what they believe is an abuser (Don), he/she was a victim of domestic violence, either as a child or an adult, or the officers called to the scene just misused their power in fracturing Don's eye socket.

Once again police officers are people, too, and have had experiences that affect how they perform their jobs. Here the officers were lawfully present in the Wright's apartment because Sade gave consent for them to enter their apartment. The police also had a valid reason to order Don to leave the residence given Sade's 911 call. What Sade was not prepared for was Don's response to the police entering their residence and Don actually being arrested.

Don's misconception that he could not be arrested in his own residence without an arrest warrant in conjunction with his first statements to the responding officers, "What's the problem?" and "You can't arrest me without an arrest warrant", most likely led to him being a victim of EXCESSIVE FORCE. Also, there is no doubt his statement led to his arrest as opposed to being removed from the residence only. If the police are called to your residence, given consent to enter your premises and see evidence of a crime or believe a crime was committed, then you will be arrested. So, when the police ask you to leave the premises despite what the caller may say in support of you staying, you must comply and leave the premises. If you do not leave the premises, then you have just failed to comply with a lawful order, which may lead to your arrest. In Don's case, with the facts as described, he still has a claim for EXCESSIVE FORCE.

Also, it should be noted once the police are lawfully in your residence (911), and they see something illegal in plain view, you can and will be arrested. For example, in the Wright's case, had the police saw a gun or drugs someone would have been arrested, if not both parties. So, you could imagine a scenario where Don is being assaulted and Sade videos the assault while verbally protesting the misconduct. In that scenario you could see the police arresting Don for domestic violence and Sade for possession of drugs, in efforts of covering up their misconduct. Notwithstanding the above, Sade could still be arrested for disorderly conduct if she intervened by videoing or verbally protesting Don's assault.

TACTICAL NOTES:

1. You have to **BE PREPARED!** Don was ill-informed about the law. He did not "Know his Rights". Don should have said as little as possible and complied with leaving the residence. **Know the law, not what you think the law is.**

2. Sade was not prepared because she did not anticipate that Don would have a negative reaction to the police and become a victim of EXCESSIVE FORCE when the only thing she wanted was him to leave the home. Simply put, she was unprepared because she did not realize that sometimes the officers you call to protect and serve actually do more harm than good. This results in the community's reluctance to contact the police because the community fears that they may do more harm than good in certain situations.

3. Only answer questions about the incident; **do not volunteer information not related to why the police were summoned.** For instance, do not volunteer information such as admitting that you have been drinking in efforts to get a break. This information will only serve to your detriment when

the offending officer seeks to justify the EXCESSIVE FORCE used against you as he describes you as belligerent, intoxicated, irate and violent. This may be a fabrication but a fabrication for which you gave the basis by stating that you were drinking. As result of your volunteered information, the police have basis to try to substantiate their misconduct – EXCESSIVE FORCE.

4. **Do more listening than talking.** Let the police officers do the talking; listen to what is being said around you.

5. Do not volunteer information because that information can and will be used against you.

6. Recognize there is no true rule of thumb as to when to speak and what to say but part of being prepared is knowing all your options as well as your lack of options in any given situation.

7. Preparation for an UNLAWFULL POLICE STOP or EXCESSIVE FORCE, includes having several strong relationships in your life: God, family, attorney, community-based leader/organization or politician.

Having a relationship with an attorney does not mean retaining an attorney where there is a financial obligation on your part but rather having someone you can contact if or when you are a victim of an UNLAWFUL POLICE STOP or EXCESSIVE FORCE. Having a relationship with an attorney is always an advantage. The fact that you have an attorney's card in your possession can deescalate an UNLAWFUL POLICE STOP if an officer were to search you and see the card. At that moment the offending officer is put on notice as to the repercussions of his misconduct, such as you choosing to file a complaint or a lawsuit. During the unfolding events, seeking an attorney for the first time may prove to be overwhelming. Additionally, it is way too late to look for an attorney when you are amid fighting for your rights.

8. BE PREPARED means anticipating that you can be the subject of an UNLAWFUL POLICE STOP or EXCESSIVE FORCE. BE PREPARED means having the ability to place the offending officers on notice that their misconduct will not go unnoticed. BE PREPARED means having an attorney that can guide your efforts in seeking the proper redress against the offending officers. You should always have your attorney's business card on your person; you will be surprised at the reaction you receive as the police search your wallet and see an attorney's card. It is likely you will notice a sharp reaction and a change in conduct once the offending officers realize you have an attorney. My personal experience and as a civil rights attorney serve as a factual base that, 80% of the time, the offending officers will seek to minimize their misconduct or role in said misconduct. The involved officers, once alerted to the fact you have legal representation, will reveal the names of those involved and will emphatically alienate themselves from the offending officers.

In some cases, to shield themselves from liability, they will inform you they had nothing to do with the unfolded events and they were just assigned the arrest. You may also be informed of the real culprits, such as the offending officers' names or shields.

9. If you are arrested and put through the system (processed), then you want to have the ability to call an attorney like you would a family physician if you were sick. Having a relationship with an attorney is critical during the arrest process. Being arrested is just like being admitted into a hospital in that if no one calls the precinct on your behalf to see what's going on then, it is likely, you will not receive immediate or proper treatment. A lawyer is your advocate and will ensure there is no delay in the processing of your paperwork or fingerprints and he/she will also try to ensure there is no delay in you seeing the judge or in your speedy release.

10. BE AWARE! "IF THE BLOCK IS HOT, STAY AWAY!" If you live on a hot block, recognize it is hot and act accordingly by limiting your exposure. This is part of being aware of your surroundings and what is going on in the community. Yes, you have the right to hangout and hangout with whomever you want; just be prepared to be detained if there is always police activity.

11. If you're going to video yours or another's UNLAWFUL POLICE STOP or incident of EXCESSIVE FORCE, **then be quiet**; let the video serve as the witness. No play by play commentary,

talking over or throughout the entire video. Talking over the video doesn't allow the attorney to hear what is being said between the victim of the UNLAWFUL POLICE STOP or victim of EXCESSIVE FORCE and the offending police officers. Remember part of being prepared is remaining composed so that you can retrieve as much information as possible from the offending officers by listening rather than speaking.

12. Additionally, if you're a victim of EXCESSIVE FORCE, always request medical treatment or request to go the hospital despite the officers telling you if you do not go to the hospital you can see the judge sooner. Going to the hospital at this early stage is the first instance where an objective third party, the hospital staff, can observe the effects of the EXCESSIVE FORCE. Moreover, have your voice heard. Always request to speak to hospital staff or the doctor to inform them how you sustained the injuries. Give your version of what occurred whether you were asked or not because most hospital staff will only record what the escorting officers say occurred. I am sure that version does not coincide with your experience. Do not let this opportunity slip away; be prepared to wait for justice.

13. **Plan your work and then work your plan.** If you are fortunate and have a friend present when you are unlawfully stopped, then work the plan that you planned to work. Stick to the plan when detained. Your objective is to get all the information you can when stopped. Do not let the circumstances throw

you off your plan. My best friend Ted and I had a plan that if we were ever unlawfully stopped, he would remember the first three numbers and I the last two of an officer's shield. He always had the assignment of remembering the first three just in case there were more than five numbers. This plan ensured that we could track down the offending officers. We focused on the officer that did the most talking. If the shield/badge numbers are concealed, then we look to the number on the RMP/police car or license plates, which will ultimately reveal the offending officers' identity. All patrol cars are assigned to a certain officer, thus leaving a direct trail to your offender. Each police car must be logged out with the time of the logging and log in upon return. This vehicle log book will reveal or confirm the identity of the offending officer.

CHAPTER 6

WHY AM I BEING ARRESTED?

It was ladies' night out and all was well after dancing and flirting at the club until Lisa noticed a young kid being abused by the police. They were surrounding the poor kid and they threw him onto the hood of a car.

Lisa tried to intervene when she yelled,
Stop abusing him!"

The police told her to
"Mind your fucking business."

Lisa in turn told the police that it was her business and to get him off the hood of her car. The police then turned their focus onto Lisa and her friends. The police officers ordered Lisa and her friends to produce their IDs. All four ladies refused to present their IDs and Lisa again requested that the officers move away from her car. One of the ladies, Sheila, called 911 and requested assistance. She told the 911 operator that they were being harassed by two males.

The responding officers, immediately seeing the two males where officers upon their arrival, requested the ladies IDs. When Sheila and Lisa questioned why it was necessary to produce their IDs, they were forcibly grabbed and pulled closely to one of the responding officers while they were told, "We ask the questions, not you!" Sheila and Lisa then provided the officers their IDs. Bailey, however, stepped back as one officer attempted to search her (patted her down). When Bailey stepped back, she was grabbed by her hair and forcibly slammed onto Lisa's car.

Tracey observing the UNLAWFUL POLICE STOP and EXCESSIVE FORCE started crying as her bag was snatched and her ID retrieved by the arriving officers. This was an illegal search of her property. Notwithstanding the fact the ladies did nothing illegal, they were all arrested for disorderly conduct, obstructing governmental administration and resisting arrest. Unlike targets of an UNLAWFUL POLICE STOP or EXCESSIVE FORCE, Lisa, Shelia, Bailey and Tracey were witnesses to EXCESSIVE FORCE, police brutality and abuse. Lisa, Shelia, Bailey or Tracey did not know whether the kid being arrested had actually committed a crime or not. Lisa observed EXCESSIVE FORCE by the police taking place on her property in public and spoke up. As a result of her protest, she became the subject of focus for the officers.

Given the above facts, you might ask yourself, what about the ladies' conduct was disorderly or how did they obstruct the police from performing their job? Lisa, Shelia, Bailey and Tracey were not being disorderly, nor did they obstruct the officers from performing their job; they simply requested that the police stop abusing the person under arrest and that the police remove themselves from Lisa's car. None of the ladies' conduct was disorderly. Lisa's verbal request did not equate to disorderly conduct or obstruction of governmental administration, unless you believe asserting your First Amendment Right to Free Speech is a crime.

Here, Lisa and her girlfriends failed to understand that their right to free speech was not helping the situation and any hostile or sarcastic communication as well as any expression of annoyance would only escalate the matter and lead to more hostility, sarcasm and annoyance by the police. More importantly, the ladies' actions would lead to an arrest for disorderly conduct, obstructing governmental administration and resisting arrest. Shelia did recognize the communication between Lisa and the officers was headed toward the worst and thus called for police assistance. Also, Sheila was wise not to state to the 911 operator that the males were police officers because it is unlikely that assistance would have responded to the location.

Sheila's call accomplished a couple of things:

- The 911 call creates an official record of the incident;

- The 911 Operator serves as an ear witness to the event unfolding given Shelia described to the operator the need for police assistance;

- The arriving/responding officers, depending upon their sense of duty to protect and serve, can intervene first or serve as actual witnesses to the incident.

- Sheila's 911 call allowed her to establish the identities of the officers involved by giving the 911 Operator the date, time and location of the incident for which any attorney can later track all of the officers involved.

If the ladies did not commit a crime, then how could they be charged with Resisting Arrest? The answer to this question is . . . the Resisting Arrest charges are bogus. What can Sheila and her friends expect given their UNLAWFUL POLICE STOP results in an arrest? The police will undoubtedly conduct a warrant check. A warrant check is when the police take your personal information (name, DOB, address and social security number), also known as Pedigree, and said Pedigree is entered into a National Database to detect if you have any outstanding warrants. You will also be fingerprinted and those fingerprints will be entered into the same database to verify if you have any outstanding warrants. A warrant can consist of failing to appear in court on another pending or old case (criminal or family court) or failing to pay a fine, court cost or child support. The database also reveals any prior arrest history.

In most cases, if you have a warrant, then you will be processed. You will be detained until you can see a judge to determine whether you are a flight risk and not likely to return to court. During your detention, you will either be handcuffed to a pole/bench or in a detaining cell with other detainees. It is my experience that arrested people are not treated kindly and requests are often ignored. Such requests consist of loosening the handcuffs, medical attention, using the bathroom or making a call to their employer or family member. In a case like that of Lisa and company, their handcuffs may be tightened to punish them for "interfering" with police business. You will be searched again at the Precinct and possibly strip-searched depending upon the punitive nature of the officers.

You will wait, wait and wait until the offending officers see fit to transport you to the court so that you can be presented before a judge. In some states, you may never see the judge. Rather, you have to wait until the offending officers call the judge on duty to make the decision on releasing you or setting bail. Duly note, if a judge is only on call and you are not presented before the court with proper legal representation then the offending officer controls the narrative articulated to the judge; you are not afforded the opportunity to speak. If you are so fortunate to receive a summons, which also is known in New York as a desk appearance ticket (DAT), while being detained at the Precinct, then you will still be detained for an unjust period but not as long if you were going to be processed.

Whether you are falsely charged and put through the system (Processed), or falsely charged and issued a summons/DAT, the false charges will consist of the following:

1. Disorderly Conduct/Disorderly Person;

2. Obstruction of Governmental Administration; and

3. Resisting Arrest.

In most states, you are allowed a phone call, and this is when having a relationship with an attorney is critical. The attorney can serve as your advocate or the liaison between you and the police/judge. The attorney can ensure you receive proper care and serve as a witness to the length of time you were detained before seeing the judge or released upon receiving a summons/DAT. Additionally, your attorney can call family members on your behalf given your ability to make phone calls are limited.

*Note that if you are charged with a violation by way of a summons or DAT then your criminal record will show that you have committed a violation not a crime if you plead guilty. If you do not receive a summons or DAT, then you will be processed which consists of being fingerprinted, photographed (mug-shot) and usually detained until you can see a judge.

TACTICAL DO'S AND DON'TS TO REMEMBER:
DO'S

1. Understand despite you doing everything "Right" from a humanitarian respective you could still be arrested.

2. Understand calling 911 for assistance may not mean that you actually receive assistance, especially when you are calling to complain about other police officers.

3. Understand you will be subjected to punitive behavior such as the tightening of handcuffs or being processed and not afforded the courtesy of a summons/DAT to avoid the humiliation of actually going to jail.

4. Work to de-escalate any hostility in the environment. Shelia attempted to have other officers present during the incident when she sensed escalation on the part of the initial officers; this was an attempt to de-escalate the situation.

5. Request the presence of a female officer if you think you will be searched at the location.

DON'TS

1. Do not say anything to the person being arrested; rather, focus on the police's actions.

2. Do not make instigating comments to your friends knowing the officers can hear you.

3. Do not expect the officers who arrive as a result of your 911 call to be on your side. The "Blue Wall of Silence" (alleged code among officers) is too strong. They will not intervene.

CHAPTER 7

"WHO SHOULD REPRESENT ME?"

Sometimes the lawyer cannot pursue a case against the police if the victim pleads guilty. Anna learned this the hard way as she left my office after a consultation. On or about October 4th 2004 at 6:00 p.m., Anna was lawfully driving down Castle Hill Avenue, Bronx, New York when she was "UNLAWFULLY" ordered by the police to pull her vehicle over. Anna complied with this order and stopped her vehicle at the nearest corner. Anna was ordered out of her car, to which she also complied, and her car was searched without her consent. Thus, the search was "UNLAWFUL" and clearly against police policies and procedures.

Anna was never informed why she was being detained and, to prevent any escalation of the situation, did not inquire but rather complied with the offending officer's orders because she did nothing illegal. Anna was also physically searched without her consent. Anna's inner thighs and breast area were searched during this so-called "Pat Down" and the present male officer placed his hands in the back pockets of her tight low rider jeans. Anna was not arrested but after a search of her vehicle, in which a box cutter and mace were recovered, she was given a summons at the precinct with a future date to return to court.

On the court date, a state provided attorney represented Anna informing her that because she had no prior arrests the prosecutor was offering a plea of guilty to a disorderly conduct or disorderly person, which is a violation and not a crime as a resolution of the matter. Anna, who wanted to sue the police for the UNLAWFUL POLICE STOP and SEARCH, did not communicate this to her state assigned attorney nor did the assigned attorney ask. Based on the facts, it was obvious the detention and search of Anna's vehicle and person was illegal but that was discarded in efforts of resolving the matter by way of plea. Anna also was concerned about having a criminal record. She was assured that her plea of guilty would not result in a criminal conviction but if the case were tried, she would not be guaranteed an acquittal. Anna was informed that the plea offer would be withdrawn if not accepted on that day. Thus, Anna entered a guilty plea to the violation, disorderly conduct.

As Anna sat in my office and I told her we cannot sue the police for their misconduct because of her guilty plea, Anna became visibly upset, eyes filled with water, face red and head bowed. Anna cried and stated, "I know I shouldn't have taken a plea, but my lawyer said it would be okay because it's not a crime; it's just a violation." Anna then confessed she also took the plea because she did not want to come back to court and miss any more days of work.

I explained to Anna if you are looking to sue the police department for violating your rights, concerning an UNLAWFUL POLICE STOP and, in this instance, an ILLEGAL SEARCH, then a guilty plea of any kind would not be in your best interest. I further explained that if you are looking to sue the police for violating your rights then you need to tell the state assigned attorney your intention and not accept any guilty plea. At the very least you should inform the attorney of your intentions and ask what, if any, effects does entering any guilty plea have on your right to sue the police for the UNLAWFUL POLICE STOP. You should not enter a plea without completely understanding "ALL" of the consequences.

- *Shame on the lawyer for not fully explaining to Anna that her case had a legitimate basis for a civil lawsuit against the police for their UNLAWFUL POLICE STOP AND SEARCH.*

- *Shame on Anna for not communicating her intentions and understanding that taking a plea of guilty (wrong doing) would not be advantageous to suing the police for the illegal stop.*

- *Shame on Anna for not wanting to come back to court to ensure she was vindicated.*

I informed Anna that I could not proceed with a lawsuit or even a complaint to the Precinct given her plea. Anna then stated she knew she should have found a "Paid Lawyer". I understood Anna's statement to mean she should have retained a private attorney who would not have let her plead guilty. Thereby, Anna would have been afforded the opportunity to decide whether she wanted to file a complaint or a lawsuit. It is important to understand the different entities for which attorneys are employed.

The entities are usually as follows:

1. Legal Aid Society (Legal Aid Lawyer);

2. Neighborhood Defenders (Public Defender);

3. 18B Lawyer (A lawyer who is appointed by the courts but maintains a private practice); and

4. Paid Lawyer (Private/Retained Attorney).

Based on your personal income, in New York, the court will assign you a legal aid attorney, neighborhood defender or an 18B attorney as your legal counsel.

Let's define each title and their role in your legal representation. First, note the aforementioned are attorneys/lawyers. They have received a formal education in law and can practice in any state, if they pass that state's bar exam. Second, their mission should be to represent you, protect you and get you released on your own recognizance (No-Bail-No Money Down). "Released on your own Recognizance" (ROR) means getting a "Get out of Jail Free Card", whereupon you can leave the courtroom without having any financial obligations or conditions relating to your release. Such conditions consist of a curfew or weekly reporting to the probation office during the pendency of your case in efforts of guaranteeing your return to court. If the court decides not to release you on your own recognizance, then the court can issue bail or remand. Bail is when you must give the court money as a condition of your release to ensure that you will return on your next court date. However, if you fail to return to court on the assigned date, then you will lose that money. On the other hand, remand means that there are no conditions the court is satisfied with to allow you to remain at liberty during the pendency of your case. In the case of remand, you will not be at liberty but rather detained until your criminal matter is resolved.

The difference between legal aid, neighborhood defender, 18B and private attorney is as follows:

A legal aid attorney and neighborhood defender/ public defender work for an agency in which each attorney receives a salary and the agency receives state or federal funding / grants to operate. The more cases they handle, the better equipped these agencies are to petition the state/federal government for more money, in efforts of recruiting more attorneys or staff to better represent you. My understanding is that the legal aid society and neighborhood defenders are one in the same as it relates to criminal defense matters; however, they receive funding from different sources.

An 18B attorney or private attorney do not work for an agency but rather themselves. However, there is a difference in that an 18B attorney (assigned court attorney) is compensated by the state on an hourly basis. At the end of the case, the 18B attorney must submit a time sheet to the court and the court/judge must approve the hours worked and compensation received by that attorney. The private/ retained attorney receives his compensation/attorney fees directly from you by way of a retainer agreement, negotiated between you and the private/retained attorney. A private attorney (retained/"paid lawyer") is hopefully someone you have a history with or referred to you by someone you trust or with whom you have a relationship.

The common perception is that legal aid and neighborhood defenders attorneys represent you less diligently than an 18B or private attorney. This perception is not always the reality. The reality is there are good and not so good and bad attorneys in every category. Whether it is legal aid, neighborhood defenders, 18B or a retained/paid attorney, you will have to let your life experiences guide you as to whether or not the attorney assigned to you is actually diligently and zealously working on your behalf. If you feel that there is not a right fit between you and your attorney, then you can always ask the court to assign you another attorney. However, it must be noted most courts will only allow one or two replacements before the court declines your request and requires you to retain private counsel – paid attorney.

The first mission of any attorney is to ensure your freedom with the least amount of restrictions or obligations on your part. That mission is accomplished when you are before the judge and he/she releases you on your own recognizance (no bail). This decision is made at arraignments (your first official court appearance). An arraignment is the first time you appear before a judge and in many cases in an UNLAWFUL POLICE STOP or EXCESSIVE FORCE scenario you will be informed of the false charges filed against you. Such false charges usually consist of "resisting arrest, disorderly conduct, and obstruction of governmental administration". If you do not have a retained/paid attorney to represent you at your arraignment, then the court will appoint a legal aid, neighborhood defenders or 18B attorney.

Prior to going before the judge, you may be afforded the opportunity to speak with your attorney. During this first attorney-client meeting, you once again must be prepared to do the one thing, which is not taught, and that is **LISTEN**. **LISTEN** to your advocate; get their business card so that if you choose to hire a private attorney the private attorney can know who to call to retrieve your criminal paperwork/information. Be prepared to **LISTEN** to a different fact scenario than what truly occurred. Be prepared to **LISTEN** to how you were the aggressor, villain or the cause for your arrest.

Depending upon how ridiculous the police's version of the facts are, you and your attorney can both decide whether it is worth informing the court what really occurred and led to your "false" arrest. A majority of the time, the police version of the facts has so many inconsistencies that the court in its infinite wisdom does not need to hear from your attorney and you are released ROR. However, in some cases it is necessary to **"Be Heard to Be Free"**, in efforts of exposing the police misconduct and to be released ROR.

The importance of an arraignment is not only to secure your freedom but also to **LISTEN** to what is presented by the prosecutor so that you can have a clear understanding of the police's false narrative, which led to your arrest. **REMEMBER TO LISTEN, RETAIN INFORMATION AND RETRIEVE INFORMATION!**

Arraignments are also critical because it is the first time the judge will have the opportunity to judge you via the presence of your family. If possible, you should never be presented before a judge without having your family present in the courtroom. A family presence illustrates to the judge you have a family support network that can assure you will return to court without any conditions such as bail or curfew. Additionally, it reveals that you have a caring support network awaiting your safe return home. In my experience, the facts of your criminal matter and your personal background are the best indicators as to whether you will be released on your own recognizance (ROR), released on bail or "remanded" (held in jail without bail). Having an overwhelming family presence in the courtroom can heavily influence a judge's decision as to bail at your arraignment. Make your presence felt. It is just like being hospitalized; the more visitors who come to visit you, the more likely you will receive favorable treatment from the nurses and the doctors. Your family members should be present not only to show support and ensure fair treatment but also to listen to what is being said about your case, retrieve information surrounding the circumstances of your case, and retain information concerning your case. Police and court personnel often talk about the upcoming cases before the court and their version of what occurred. This is an appropriate time for your family members to **"ear hustle"**, which can serve to your advantage when you file a complaint or lawsuit.

The issue faced by most families is whether to use their monetary resources to secure a good retained/paid attorney in hopes of getting you released with no financial obligations to the court or use those same funds for bail, anticipating that bail will be warranted, and proceed with a court appointed attorney, legal aid, neighborhood defenders or 18B. Depending upon the alleged criminal charges, your personal criminal history, if any, and the relationship you have developed with your family attorney will determine how you use your resources. Each decision is fact sensitive and there is no rule of thumb. If you do not have a personal relationship with an attorney at the time of your false arrest, then your family can do the research while you are waiting to be presented at your arraignment. They can see if a retained/paid attorney can be secured to represent you or proceed with a court appointed attorney as previously discussed.

TACTICAL NOTES:

- REMEMBER TO LISTEN

- RETAIN INFORMATION

- RETRIEVE INFORMATION

CHAPTER 8

"WILL YOU TAKE MY CASE?"

It has been my experience that sometimes, although a person's rights may have been violated, they still may not have a potential lawsuit. Factors used in evaluating whether or not a set of facts are ripe for a lawsuit are the facts themselves, nature of the injury and the criminal history of the victim. The scenario below illustrates the vetting process in deciding whether to file a false arrest or excessive force lawsuit.

Big Ed was walking through a park, taking a shortcut. It was late at night and the park is known for being a place where you can be robbed but Big Ed was not worried. As he entered the park, two undercover police officers walked past. Big Ed realized they were cops, but he ignored their presence. As Big Ed neared the middle of the park, two White-Hispanic undercover officers approached him and ordered him to take his hands out of his pants pocket. Big Ed complied. Big Ed was then requested to show ID. Once again Big Ed complied. At this point, without warning, one police officer attempted to handcuff Big Ed. They yanked his arms behind his back; he did not resist but knew they would not be able to cuff him using one set of handcuffs because he is so broad. He said nothing. The officers hit him in the stomach with an expandable metal baton forcing him to the ground. Big Ed was ordered to go to his knees, although crouched over in pain. They hit Big Ed a couple of more times creating some swelling and bruises. Finally, the offending officers realized they needed two sets of cuffs because Big Ed is so big.

The officers took Big Ed to an unmarked police van and sat him down. They informed Big Ed that he fit the description of a robber and that they were waiting for a confirmed ID by the victim. Big Ed remained seated, handcuffed behind his back for 45 minutes. The alleged victim was presented to make an identification of "Big Ed" as his assailant. This identification is called a "Show-Up" identification procedure. No positive show-up identification was established (no street identification by the victim). Big Ed then was transported to the local precinct where he was detained while still handcuffed and held overnight to see a judge in the morning. However, in the morning he was let out the back door. Big Ed was shocked but calm upon his release from the precinct. Though Big Ed sustained minor injuries, his case still presented grounds for a potential lawsuit.

Big Ed told me the above story at his consultation. After hearing his story, I asked him did he have a prior criminal history. Big Ed stated he did have prior convictions for robbery, gun possession and resisting arrest/disorderly conduct. The question then became should I take his case and commence a lawsuit. My answer was no, and these were the reasons why:

1. Big Ed's injuries were not permanent which correlates to the monetary value of his case. The more severe the injury, the greater the financial settlement/award. Therefore, based on Big Ed's particular facts, I assessed this case as an EXCESIVE FORCE case exclusively. I decided not to manage his case (a business decision, not a moral decision). Undoubtedly, Big Ed was a victim of EXCESSIVE FORCE. However, every case of EXCESSIVE FORCE is not a great case to litigate and Big Ed's scenario is a prime example. It should be noted, Big Ed's facts did not lend itself to a FALSE ARREST lawsuit because a third party (civilian) gave a description that matched Big Ed, although the show up identification was negative.

2. Big Ed has a prior criminal record, which would be revealed at trial and most people will not overlook his prior criminal convictions. Most people do not want to financially reward a criminal and sometimes it is irrelevant how long ago the crimes occurred in the past.

Morally, I would have wanted to take Big Ed's case because Big Ed was a victim of EXCESSIVE FORCE; however, I must balance managing cases grounded on "Principle against cases with a Principle return." Based on this business motto, each case must be examined and evaluated separately. By no means am I suggesting a past criminal record precludes someone from commencing a FALSE ARREST or EXCESSIVE FORCE lawsuit, but it is a factor that every attorney takes into consideration. An evaluation and conversation about who you are in totality must be had and taken into consideration before pursuing a lawsuit. This evaluation process helps identify the various outcomes of a lawsuit. Big Ed's past criminal history does not excuse the offending officers use of EXCESSIVE FORCE nor should his past criminal history justify an UNLAWFUL POLICE STOP. Usually at the time of the UNLAWFUL POLICE STOP, the police officers are unaware of your past criminal history, (if any), present occupation or whether you are a good guy. These descriptions are not stamped on your forehead at the time of the UNLAWFUL POLICE STOP or EXCESSIVE FORCE INCIDENT. In Big Ed's case I would strongly suggest that we pursue a complaint by way of the Civil Complaint Review Broad (CCRB) if he lives in New York or by filing a complaint administratively depending on the state in which he resides.

CHAPTER 9

IF I CAN'T SUE...
WHAT CAN I DO?

If you are a victim of an UNLAWFUL POLICE STOP or EXCESSIVE FORCE, what can you do to seek redress? Do you SUE? SUE WHO? The answer is the police and the City for which the police officers are employed. So, how do you do this? In New York you must file a notice of claim within 90 days of the UNLAWFUL POLICE STOP or EXCESSIVE FORCE occurrence. However, each state has different laws as to how to initiate a lawsuit against the police, municipality or sheriff's department. A good source to find the filing deadlines, also known as statute of limitations, is on the Internet. All you need to do is research statute of limitations for filing a lawsuit against the police.

The State of New York requires the filing of a notice of claim prior to the commencing of a lawsuit in the state court. This requirement is not warranted if a lawsuit is filed in federal court; however, I suggest to always file a notice of claim anyway to prevent your lawsuit from being precluded and also to have the flexibility to proceed in state court as well as in federal court. For example, in New York you have 90 days to file the notice of claim. And if you fail to file, you will be precluded from proceeding in state court. A notice of claim is a document drafted by you or your attorney, notifying the municipality, town, city or police department of your UNLAWFUL POLICE STOP or EXCESSIVE FORCE experience. The notice of claim is necessary because it is the vehicle for which you, for the first time, have articulated how your state and federal constitutional rights were violated.

If you fail to file a notice a claim or precluded from commencing a lawsuit is state court you can alternatively file your lawsuit in federal court. Pursuant to a 1983 civil rights violation cause of action, you can proceed in federal court, however there is usually a three year statute of limitations to file such a lawsuit. The Civil Rights Act of 1871 is a federal statute, (42 USC Section 1983), that allows you to sue the government for civil rights violations. Civil rights violations, pursuant to 42 USC Section 1983 applies to someone, i.e. police officers, acting as police officers under state or local law and that has deprived you of your US Constitutional Rights.

TACTICAL NOTES:

1. NO NOTICE - NO SUIT. In rare cases, your attorney may be able to overcome missing the ninety (90) day deadline by showing "GOOD CAUSE" explaining why you missed the ninety (90) day notice of claim deadline. An example of "GOOD CAUSE" is hospitalization, death of a significant other and sometimes human error if you filed the notice of claim on the 91st day.

2. Do not wait until your criminal case is dismissed before filing the notice of claim. Usually, when you are a victim of an UNLAWFUL POLICE STOP or EXCESSIVE FORCE, you are also arrested. "Good Cause" does not include waiting until your criminal case is dismissed. You cannot wait until your criminal case is dismissed because usually the case will take more than ninety days to resolve itself.

3. If you plan to sue, then you must realize you cannot enter a plea of any kind unless you are just suing exclusively for EXCESSIVE FORCE. For example, if you were observed urinating in the public (a quality of life crime), and as result of your arrest you sustain a dislocated knee, then you have a great EXCESSIVE FORCE case. In this case a guilty plea is irrelevant because you are not claiming false arrest but rather the use of EXCESSIVE FORCE. The use of EXCESSIVE FORCE is a state and federal constitutional violation. Another example would be if you were observed smoking marijuana and the police stop you, and in the process of your arrest, the officers batter and assault you, resulting in bruising and swelling. Again, a plea of guilty to smoking marijuana is irrelevant. The plea to smoking marijuana is irrelevant because you are not alleging that the stop and arrest was unlawful but rather the force used was excessive and because of the EXCESSIVE FORCE used, your state and federal constitutional rights were violated.

4. After the filing of a notice of claim, preserving your right to sue, you now have one year from the date of the incident to file certain legal causes of

actions, like battery and assault, personally against the offending police officers, noting every state has different deadlines to file these legal causes of action mentioned. Some attorneys, in New York, abide by the 190-day rule to file a lawsuit. It is because of these various statutes of limitations (deadlines) that hiring an attorney is warranted.

5. If you are precluded from filing a lawsuit, still notify your local, state and federal elected representatives.

6. Be smart; hire an attorney. If you miss these deadlines, then you are "S.O.L." Be smart; hire an attorney.

Now you may say to yourself hiring an attorney costs money; that's not correct in all cases. In civil rights cases for FALSE ARREST/EXCESSIVE FORCE, most, if not all, attorneys take these cases on a contingency. A contingency case is one in which an attorney will accept the case and incur all expenses in exchange for 33% of the award you receive. Additionally, the attorney will be allowed to recoup his/her expenses. Usually the contingent fee is 33% plus expenses incurred at settle or the end of trial. A settlement is a resolution without a trial before a jury and negotiated by the attorneys. A trial is when witnesses are necessary to testify before a jury and the jury determines liability and financial compensation if any. Expenses usually include securing medical records, medical experts, and filing fees as it pertains to filing the lawsuit. Other expenses include officially serving the parties involved with the lawsuit, filing fee for pleadings, and motions to ensure the case is not dismissed. Excluding the above, the remaining of the settlement is yours. Once your summons and complaint is filed, you are on your way to seeking redress for the police misconduct.

Nothing will motivate change as quickly as hitting the City in the pocket for negligence in hiring these POWER COPS, CLASSIST COPS, PREJUDICED COPS OR CREATING QUOTA COPS. In addition to filing a lawsuit, holding rallies and staging boycotts are effective ways to be heard on issues of false arrest or police brutality. One should also write to his/her own city, state or federal representatives and have them consider legislation to ensure that the offending police officers are held accountable for their misconduct. The long-term goal is to have **LEGISLATIVE CHANGE** as it relates to policing and this can only occur when your city, state and federal representatives are engaged, as well as advocacy organizations such as **National Action Network (NAN), Justice League NYC, Justice Committee, 100 Blacks in Law Enforcement Who Care and Cop Watch**.

Holding the offending police officers financially liable would be one form of **LEGISLATIVE REFORM.** Imagine if when you settle a case for $250,000.00 the offending officers involved have to pay a portion of the settlement or award. This would undoubtedly curb or deter abusive behavior/police misconduct in the future. As they say "Money talks . . ." and having financial accountability will definitely change the police officer's behavior. New York City in the past 5 years has paid approximately 384 million dollars to settle cases of police misconduct as reported in the NY Post Article "NYC Has Shelled Out 384 Million in 5 Years To Settle NYPD Suits, September 4, 2018." Settlements for low level misconduct have ranged from $5000 – $25,000. What is interesting about this statement is what some have described as low level misconduct is often devastating for the victim of the misconduct. Residency requirement is another legislative suggestion to create a community policing environment, whereupon relations are built. Relationships are built on trust, respect and transparency between the police and communities of color for whom the police are employed to protect and serve. It is this type of **LEGISLATIVE CHANGE** you should be pushing for in your community to ensure justice and fair treatment under the law.

CHAPTER 10

IS IT WORTH IT?

Often victims of police misconduct choose not to pursue a lawsuit for a variety of reasons. My experience has revealed that the reasons for not pursuing a lawsuit may vary. Some people feel an UNLAWFUL POLICE STOP or EXCESSIVE FORCE is a way of life; some people think the misconduct was not that serious; some people do not have the time or want to make the time; and some people just do not know what the steps are to pursue a lawsuit.

No matter what the reason(s), you should file some type of complaint, if possible. Some police precincts allow "Walk-in complaints". This occurs when a victim of police misconduct walks into a precinct and is afforded the opportunity to speak with a Lieutenant or Sergeant to file an internal complaint. Upon meeting with the Lieutenant or Sergeant, an interview is conducted for which a complaint is filed against the offending officer(s). In this scenario, it is quite possible an internal investigation will occur, and you will be excluded from the process and may not be notified of the results.

In New York City, an independent agency, Civil Complaint Review Board (hereafter referred as CCRB), serves as an agency for which victims of police misconduct can file a complaint. CCRB was created to ensure that your case will be investigated and you are involved in the process as well as informed of the outcome.

There was a time when I viewed CCRB as an agency beholden to the New York City Police Department but over time this view has changed. What substantiated this opinion were the numerous cases of police misconduct for which the CCRB concluded there was no misconduct. CCRB would often times agree with the police and not hold the police accountable for their misconduct. A substantiated finding from a CCRB investigation speaks volume because it validates the alleged misconduct, which will result in some discipline. Again, over time CCRB has been varied in its investigations and findings, however, CCRB has displayed more independence and vigor in its investigations.

Even if an investigation results in an unsubstantiated finding, the fact that there was an investigation for misconduct is extremely important. The filing of a complaint is important because it creates a record/history of the offending officer(s) which is recorded and maintained in his professional-personnel employment file and will forever follow him while he maintains employment as a police officer. The offending officer's professional history, inclusive of any filed complaints for misconduct, establishes that the city/ municipality was put on "notice" of said misconduct and failed to discipline or retrain the offending officer(s). Thus, as a result the offending officer(s) continues his illegal conduct. In cases where the police department does discipline or retrain the offending officer(s) and he continues his illegal conduct, this behavior illustrates that the disciplinary actions failed as deterrence or the retraining was ineffective.

Just imagine being a victim of an UNLAWFUL POLICE STOP or EXCESSIVE FORCE only to discover during your lawsuit, the offending officers have a history of misconduct similar in nature to your experience. This information would expediently fortify your claim of negligence, failure to train, failure to discipline or deliberate indifference as to the offending officer's misconduct. Your negligence cause of action is strengthened because the law enforcement agency failed to address the prior misconduct. Your failure to train and discipline causes of actions, are also strengthened. The repeated misconduct illustrates a lack of training/retraining or a failure to discipline in order to deter said misconduct. Lastly, if the law enforcement agency did nothing at all to discipline or train/retrain the offending officer's conduct, then they deliberately showed indifference to said misconduct.

Although prior *"notice"* of the offending officer's misconduct is not required to initiate a complaint or lawsuit, it assists in establishing the city's/municipality's *"negligence"* or *"deliberate indifference"*. Negligence is defined as the failure to take proper care resulting in damage or injury to another. Deliberate indifference is defined as ignoring a situation known to exist. In rare incidents, the Internal Affairs Bureau (IAB) of a police department will initiate an UNLAWFUL POLICE STOP or EXCESSIVE FORCE investigation. IAB is a self-regulating division of the police department. **Note you still must file a notice of claim within the 90-day deadline.**

Given IAB is the police departments' self-regulating investigative unit, a finding of culpability or a recommendation for retraining or disciplinary action is rare to non-existent. My experience with IAB has taught me that relying on IAB to assist in establishing misconduct of one of their fellow colleagues will only lead to frustration and their investigation will serve as an opportunity to create a defense to justify the offending officer's misconduct. IAB has rarely substantiated culpability in cases involving UNLAWFUL POLICE STOP, EXCESSIVE FORCE and "WRONGFUL DEATH"; the results are the same: no culpability and no termination. Although IAB investigations are not public information, once again, said investigations are a permanent part of the offending officer's personnel/professional employment file. This information can be obtained during the exchange of documents upon initiating a lawsuit.

NO INDIVIDUAL SHOULD TOLERATE POLICE MISCONDUCT! The New York Police Department's motto is "RESPECT, COURTESY and PROFESSIONALISM." My professional experience leads me to conclude that people of color often encounter "DISRESPECT, DISCOURTESY and UNPROFESSIONALISM" when confronted by police officers. My personal and professional experience also leads me to conclude people of color do not hold police to the standard of treating them with RESPECT, COURTESY and PROFESSIONALISM by not filing complaints regarding any misconduct suffered, such as being "DISCOURTEOUS."

Every experience of police misconduct should be officially documented. By documenting the misconduct, a case can be made for negligence, racial profiling, implicit bias in training, deliberate indifference and negligence in hiring and failure to train/retrain offending officers. Filing a complaint creates a paper trail of misconduct and is an effective way to create change in how our communities are policed. We the community serve as the "CHECKS and BALANCES" of the police and the Judicial system in its totality.

Discussing possible remedies to ensure communities or individuals' civil/human rights are not violated should always be at the forefront of police reform. Such remedies are residency requirements for members of the service or prorated financial penalties if the offending officer is proven to be liable as well as creating laws (like Right to Know Act) and policies that lead to transparency.

CHAPTER 11

WHY DIDN'T YOU SAY ANYTHING?

J.A., Clift and Blaise were riding in J.A father's BMW SUV on their way to the mall. J.A. and Clift are Caucasian teenagers and Blaise is an African American teenager. They all attend the same private high school in the suburbs. Minutes away from the mall they were stopped by the town police. J.A. knows he was not speeding so the two other passengers continued texting and talking prior to being stopped. When stopped J.A. complied with the officer's request. It should be noted the officers were males and both Caucasian. J.A. complied and forwarded his driver's license, insurance card and registration. Clift sarcastically stated, "We were not speeding, so what's the deal?" The detaining officers did not respond. Blaise sat alone in the back-passenger seats legs stretched out across the seats and on his phone surfing a variety of social media outlets.

After one officer returned from his vehicle, he gave J.A. a ticket for his bumper guard blocking his license plate. J.A. protested the ticket and Clift commented that the stop was "Bullshit". Blaise remained quiet; he did not say a word or even cough. Upon returning with the ticket, the officer requested that Blaise exit the vehicle. Blaise again said nothing but complied against the advice of both of his friends. J.A. and Clift said, "Blaise don't get out; remain seated – you did nothing wrong." They also stated that the officer's request was racially motivated and "We know our rights." Blaise, nonetheless, silently exited the vehicle, whereupon he was stared at from head to toe. Blaise was not searched or requested to go to the back of the vehicle, but he was observed with no exchanging of words. Blaise stood outside of the vehicle for less than a minute as they observed him. He also observed their faces, badge numbers and demeanor before asking that they call his parents or if he could he call his parents. Blaise did not assess whether he was dealing with a QUOTA COP, POWER COP, PREJUDICED COP OR CLASSIST COP. What he did know was to request to speak to his parents immediately with confidence in his voice. After his request, he was free to go, as J.A. and Clift just watched. No recording or texting to their parents occurred as Blaise stood outside of the vehicle. J.A. and Clift just watched as if they were watching a documentary on false arrest/police brutality. When Blaise re-entered the car, they both asked, *"Why didn't you say anything during the entire incident except for requesting to call your parents?"*

Blaise explained although he was not the subject of the stop, he believed he may have become the focus of attention during the stop and silence served him best as not to become the focus of their attention. Blaise knew saying nothing while in the car served his best interest. He was not driving, so why assert himself to become the focus of attention? Blaise also knew having him exit the car was done to harass and provoke a hostile and negative response. Blaise was socially, and racially, educated enough on how to manage an UNLAWFUL POLICE STOP and that silence was best. Blaise understood that the luxuries to voice his First Amendment Right of Free Speech would not be the best option and actually silence was more empowering. Blaise's silence was empowering because it gave the officers no overt reason to continue to harass or arrest Blaise. It put on display the officers' misconduct in abusing their power. Blaise did not verbalize his frustration, anxiety or feeling of being scared; he complied while also requesting the presence of his parents. Despite his friends' verbal protest, Blaise did not join in; that was a smart thing to do.

This UNLAWFUL POLICE STOP lasted less than five minutes and neither of the boys talked about it after being ordered to leave. Blaise never said anything to his parents. They found out weeks later by way of J.A.'s parents at a football game; just imagine his parent's shock.

Blaise's ability to remain composed has afforded him the opportunity to file a complaint or lawsuit. The only obstacle was his delay in telling his parents about the incident. Blaise was able to retrieve the important information, such as the offending officers' name and badge number. He was not the subject of the stop because he was not the driver; therefore, there was no basis to have him exit the vehicle or make an arrest. Blaise realized that he did not have the same "Freedom of Speech" liberties as his Caucasian friends.

I can only speculate as to why Blaise did not tell his parents. My own childhood experience leads me to believe that this is the norm for people of color and there was nothing to tell from his prospective. Being unlawfully detained by the police should not be the norm for anyone whether you live in the suburbs or the inner city and when it occurs your voice must be heard.

TACTICAL DO'S AND DON'TS TO REMEMBER:
DO'S

1. Request your parents be present or called before talking to the police if you are a minor and detained and questioned by the police.

2. Remain out of the attention/focus of the police if you are not the initial reason for the stop. Once again, no need to be the civil rights activist or attorney for the group.

3. Remind your friends whether Caucasian, Black or a girlfriend/boyfriend that if they are not the subject of the UNLAWFUL POLICE STOP then their verbal exchange with the police can serve to do more harm than good in any given scenario.

4. Never delay in telling your parents what occurred. There is no shame. You did nothing wrong and you must inform your parents because they are here to protect you. They will find a way to make sure your voice is heard.

DON'TS

1. Do not ignore the police request, although you think you are not the target of the UNLAWFUL POLICE STOP.

2. Do not consent to any search.

3. Do not verbalize your knowledge of the law.

4. Do not verbalize your frustration.

5. Do not avoid telling your parents about your UNLAWFUL POLICE STOP experience.

CHAPTER 12
THINK C.A.L.M.

The use of the tactical information shared in this guide may not solve all the disparities in our criminal justice system but my hope is that it will inform and empower you. Utilizing the strategies shared will hopefully increase the likelihood of your safety. More importantly, I want to empower YOU to have the tactical tools to succeed if you encounter an UNLAWFUL POLICE STOP and choose to file a complaint or lawsuit.

When you actually encounter an UNLAWFUL POLICE STOP or EXCESSIVE FORCE, I want you to remember the following phrase: **THINK C.A.L.M.** Although events may be rapidly unfolding around you when you are unlawfully detained or subjected to excessive force, you must "**THINK C.A.L.M.**"

- Stay **C**omposed,
- Be **A**ware,
- **L**isten &
- **M**ake a Call.

You must stay "**C**omposed" because if you are not composed and allow your emotions to take over then you will not be able to manage the UNLAWFUL POLICE STOP but rather the UNLAWFUL POLICE STOP will manage you. In other words do not let your emotions stand in the way of you retrieving critical information as to the police officers involved. As I stated previously, the shield number or the license plate of the police car is critical information necessary to identify the offending officers.

You must be "**A**ware" because if you are aware you can take a mental note as to whether there are business cameras located at the location where you were a subject of EXCESSIVE FORCE or an UNLAWFUL POLICE STOP. Clearly, video footage of what actually occurred can only help your case if you choose to file a lawsuit or a complaint. Be "**A**ware" as to whether the offending officers turn off their body cameras during the encounter.

You must "**L**isten" because by listening you may be able to hear the complete name of the detaining officer(s). Usually the officer's last name is on their badge so if you are listening you may be able to hear the first name, establishing another means of identification. Also if you "**L**isten" to the offending officer's orders hopefully that will decrease your exposure to any hostility as well as you may discover the reason, if any, for your stop.

You must **M**ake a call, literally if you can, and have that person serve as an ear witness. If you cannot literally make the call, then call out to bystanders; there is nothing wrong with calling out to bystanders to witness the unfolding events. There is nothing too humiliating about screaming out for help when you think your life is endangered or your civil rights are being violated. When you call out for help, ask those observing to video the incident or call your loved one, parent, spouse or friend. Videoing is legal and in NY, pursuant to the Police Patrol Guide, officers cannot prohibit you from videoing.

REMEMBER TO **THINK "C.A.L.M."** and retrieve important information so that your attorney can help you receive justice and most importantly save more lives.

NOTES